MasterClass in Drama Education

Also available from Continuum

Drama Education with Digital Technology, edited by Michael Anderson, David Cameron and John Carroll

School Improvement Through Drama, Patrice Baldwin

100 Ideas for Teaching Drama, Johnnie Young

Getting the Buggers into Drama, Sue Cowley

Inspired Drama Teaching, Keith West

Positive Placements, David Midwinter and Tracy Whatmore

MasterClass in Drama Education

Transforming Teaching and Learning

Michael Anderson

continuum

Continuum International Publishing Group

The Tower Building	80 Maiden Lane
11 York Road	Suite 704
London SE1 7NX	New York NY 10038

www.continuumbooks.com

British Library Cataloguing-in-Publication Data
A catalogue record for this book is available from the British Library.

ISBN: 978-1-4411-8589-1 (paperback)
       978-1-4411-6700-2 (hardcover)

Library of Congress Cataloging-in-Publication Data
Anderson, Michael, 1969-
MasterClass in drama education : transforming teaching and learning /
Michael Anderson.
       p. cm. — (MasterClass)
 Includes bibliographical references and index.
 ISBN 978-1-4411-8589-1 – ISBN 978-1-4411-6700-2 1. Drama–Study
and teaching. I. Title.

PN1701.A64 2011
792.071—dc23
                                                       2011016998

Typeset by Newgen Imaging Systems Pvt Ltd, Chennai, India
Printed and bound in India

For Rebecca, Henry and Thomas

Contents

Series Editor's Foreword

The MasterClass series is designed to energize the idea of education through a creative exploration of the key ideas which inform effective teaching and learning. In *MasterClass in Drama Education*, Michael Anderson has created a book which precisely responds to this demand: using narrative, he weaves accounts of his own teaching experiences and his students' learning in ways which stimulate and challenge where and how drama education can develop a pedagogy of collaborative and imaginative approaches to powerful learning.

The volume is organized into two major parts. The first, 'Drama Education for Generation Next: Foundations for Effective Pedagogy' examines the place of drama teaching in the arts within contemporary education, with a particular emphasis on collaborative learning in drama. Part 2 'Teaching Drama with Generation Next: Pedagogy in Practice' explores how future students might best be supported through classroom approaches which place drama at the centre of exciting and innovative ways of thinking about learning.

The volume is much more though than a series of strategies, although certainly these appear regularly: rather it is a thoughtful positioning of drama as a means to examine where and how education might speak more directly to our students, whose own learning worlds are so often bounded by exhortations to see education as a means to an end, often reductively measured by monetary success in the workplace, rather than any recognition of education as a means to a just and democratic society and our place within that. Anderson offers three principles which inform his view of the potential of drama: developing critical hope; equipping the field for the challenges of the twenty-first century and that drama educators need to teach 'truth telling' – the art of reflecting back realities so that we might engage and rewrite our futures through education, and specifically through drama. As Anderson says:

> That is why drama education is vital, not because it helps us do sums better or get on better with our workmates (although those things are important) but because it allows us to craft lies that tell the truth about ourselves and about our community.

In *MasterClass in Drama Education*, Anderson has created both a text to inform practice and a text to stimulate the wider and essential debates about the place of education for 'generation next'. I am delighted to be able to add this volume to the MasterClass series and to thank Michael Anderson for being a 'lighter of fires'.

Sue Brindley, Senior Lecturer in Education
University of Cambridge, UK

Acknowledgements

I would like to acknowledge all the students, teachers and other colleagues in primary, secondary and tertiary education throughout the world who have been so generous with their knowledge, wisdom and time. I would especially like to thank: Judith Ackroyd, George Belliveau, David Cameron, John Carroll, Robyn Ewing, Michael Finneran, Kelly Freebody, John Hughes, Andy Kempe, Peter O'Connor, John O'Toole, Carole Miller, Jonothan Neelands, Helen Nicholson, Juliana Saxton and Jennifer Simons. These people have been and continue to be teachers and guides to me as well as treasured colleagues.

For assistance with this book I would specifically like to thank Miranda Jefferson, Matthew Clausen and Carol Anderson.

A special thanks and acknowledgement to Alison Baker and Rosie Pattinson at Continuum who have guided and helped me through the publishing process. Thanks also to the wonderful series editor Sue Brindley who gave me the chance to write this book and supported me along the way.

Introduction

Why the arts matter

The arts matter because as Peter Abbs (2003) claim they give us the ability to live truly human, truly deep and ultimately meaningful lives:

> . . . the arts matter because they serve – at their best – the deep human impulse to understand, to integrate and to transcend; they serve life's ineradicable desire to live more fully, more abundantly. I have always felt that art and, especially, the making of art enables individuals to ratchet up their ephemeral lives to the level of high symbolic adventure and philosophical questing.

Everything in this book assumes that the arts should not only be the centre of education but also the centre of a deep and fulfilling existence.

About this book

Masterclass explores how drama teachers might face the challenges presented by a generation of young people unlike any who have gone before them. The book argues that schooling, schools and students are changing and teachers must respond to this change by transforming their approach to drama education. The chapters explore critical perspectives for drama education as they relate to the drama teacher's changing role. The book examines some of the key debates in the field and discusses strategies to engage and motivate the present and the next generation of students in drama learning. This is not necessarily a book of teaching strategies per se (although you will find strategies dotted throughout the book as examples) but an exploration of critical perspectives in drama education and an exploration of how these perspectives might transform drama teaching practice. You will notice that I employ narratives throughout. Stories are central to the way we understand lived experience. In this book they form the vital link between ideas and classroom reality. I am going to start by telling a story about one of my students, Ryan.

About Ryan

Ryan was, and for all I know is still, a football player. But not just any football player, he was the roughest football player in the school team. He spent much of his time when he was not squirrel gripping (don't ask) or eye gouging being suspended and taking 'a spell on the bench'. But strangely enough he was not cruel, he had a spark, a light that people enjoyed . . . to that extent he was somewhat a paradox. He was a tough kid and for reasons best known to him decided to study drama in my class. Ryan was what teachers might all call a 'poor student'. He was charming but he never applied himself; he mucked around endlessly, he didn't even turn up from time to time but again he was never nasty nor cruel. The time came for Ryan, as it always does, to present an individual performance at his final examination. This is a solo performance of around seven minutes, presented for three external examiners. Ryan had not shown up for the rehearsal and I feared a 'no show' or worse on the performance day. But Ryan did turn up. He walked on stage, the examiners watching and I sat there with my eyes closed peeking through the gap in my fingers wondering what, if anything, might happen next. The lights buzzed up, the audience held its breath (I had been holding mine for about an hour), and then out of the mouth of this footballer came a Louisiana accent and a piece so subtly and beautifully crafted that it made everyone weep, including the examiners. I can still remember the shock I felt and still find myself wondering how this happened. Did something seep into Ryan's head and heart in the classes he seemed to ignore? Was he a natural who was finally showing his 'other side' hidden as a defence? I really do not know and I probably cannot ever know.

These miraculous stories sustain us and although they are not enough to convince curriculum gatekeepers of our worth, they do sustain drama teachers. It is really the Ryans of this world that motivated me to write this book. I am also motivated to write for two other reasons, one old and one new. The old reason is that I believe drama is a dynamic, transformative and powerful art form that creates profound learning when taught effectively. The second reason relates to the first. We cannot if we care about the future of the field take the dynamism and transformative quality of drama learning for granted. Society including schools, teaching and learning is in flux and we cannot just expect things to be as they always have been. This book examines the foundations of our practice in Part 1 as a way to inform and assist drama educators to construct the future. Part 1, Drama Education for Generation Next: Foundations for Effective Pedagogy, discusses the place of drama teaching in the arts, the challenges that confront education and collaborative learning in drama. Section 2 Part 2, Teaching Drama with Generation Next: Pedagogy in Practice examines the implications of these foundations for real drama teachers with real students. The idea behind this book, indeed this series, is that education and learning should be debated, an interchange of ideas argued around practice and research. My hope is that the book that follows will inspire, inform and even provoke debate to make a difference for the Ryans in our classrooms and that drama will be a dynamic and an engaging place of learning for the generations of learners we see in our classrooms for years to come.

Part I
Drama Education For Generation Next: Foundations For Effective Pedagogy

Teaching Drama in the Twenty-First Century

Chapter Outline

When I graduated with my drama teaching qualifications, I thought the world might remain pretty much as it had been all my life. I thought what I had to do was simple: teach young people about the human condition through the action and language of drama and theatre. Simple. Of course what I had not considered was that the world around me would shift to become unrecognizable to me from the classroom I entered 20-odd years ago. What didn't strike me then but does now is that the changing world of our students has implications for our teaching. Fortunately, drama education has within it all the resources to cope with that change. This book examines the changing world of education and the way drama education's resources can help teachers and students alike not only to respond to change but make changes themselves – to be actors and audiences simultaneously.

In the last decade or two, there has been any number of books, articles and general pronouncements about the rate of change in society, schools and in the lives of young people. We are assured that change is upon us as a constant and that those who ignore change do so at their peril. As the British Prime Minister Harold Wilson said, 'He who rejects change is the architect of decay. The only human institution which rejects progress is the cemetery' (*The New York Times*, 24 January 1967). Indeed since the 1950s, prominent educators have been talking about the 'technological revolution and educational expansion of the last hundred years' (Connell et al., 1957, p. 207) bringing lasting change. If change is such a constant, why is there still a host of pronouncements about how profound change is and will be for the teacher and student of the twenty-first century?

I believe schools and schooling are pretty similar to the way they looked in the 1950s. While the various revolutions in ideas, culture, aesthetics, technology and politics have made the society of 2012 unrecognizable from 1912, much about our current schools and classrooms results from the demands of the industrial revolution rather than the demands of the digital revolution. School buildings built to educate baby boomers have somehow captured the demands of that generation in their fabric, in their DNA, excluding most new ideas and demands to change them. As Furlong argues:

> core aspects of the education system were designed to meet the needs of young people growing up in the 1950s. In that period, there was an emphasis on preparing young people for a relatively static occupational world in which their futures were clearly mapped out, and the skills required were well defined. This traditional model of education tends to privilege knowledge legitimized by the curriculum over learning that takes place in the community or in other contexts. As many educational sociologists have observed, education is often organized in ways that facilitate control and prepare young people for a workforce in which conformity is valued over creativity. (2009, p. iv)

Against this seeming blizzard of change in society more generally and in schools particularly, schooling and ultimately teachers and students are challenged to respond to this change. While all curriculum areas must engage with change, drama has something unique to offer the young people of today and tomorrow. Drama teachers are perhaps best placed to deal with this dynamic in their classrooms as drama allows participants to imagine and enact futures. In a sense the drama classroom is a laboratory for choices. It allows those involved in the drama to try out ideas, to give them a 'test drive' before they 'hit the highway'. Before we go too far into the how and why of drama teaching for generation next, I would like to identify some of the principles that underpin this book. I do this to acknowledge the subjectivity of my approach; I do this to recognize that any book that attempts to discuss drama education in a globalized world will fall short in some ways because of the individual contextual factors that all teachers face in their own situations. To this extent all books that purport to discuss classrooms and teaching are limited and those that pretend they are not should be treated with extreme caution. So here are some general principles that set a context about the schools and schooling systems that drama teachers work within.

The world is changing and not changing

President Obama's inauguration speech was one of the touchstone moments of the twenty-first century. At the time it was delivered, there was a hopeful but perhaps unrealistic euphoria about what might have been possible, but still the insoluble problems persist. Obama said:

> That we are in the midst of crisis is now well understood. Our nation is at war, against a far-reaching network of violence and hatred. Our economy is badly weakened, a consequence of

greed and irresponsibility on the part of some, but also our collective failure to make hard choices and prepare the nation for a new age. Homes have been lost; jobs shed; businesses shuttered. Our healthcare is too costly; our schools fail too many; and each day brings further evidence that the ways we use energy strengthen our adversaries and threaten our planet. (Obama, 2009)

In addition to these seemingly timeless challenges, many in Western societies have near universal access to knowledge through the digitization of previously difficult-to-access materials held in printed form. Andy Hargreaves argues that this has transformed our world into a 'knowledge society'. Tragically schools have not responded enthusiastically. Again they seem stuck, perhaps because of outmoded practices ignoring these changes. Instead of developing innovation and imagination, national testing regimes are wheeled in, substituting for meaningful educational reform. As Hargreaves argues,

. . . instead of fostering creativity and ingenuity, more and more school systems have become obsessed with imposing and micromanaging curriculum uniformity. In place of ambitious missions of compassion and community, schools and teachers have been squeezed into the tunnel vision of test scores, achievement targets and league tables of accountability. (2003, p. 1)

So you might be excused for thinking that in the face all these challenges and opportunities, schooling would have changed in the last decades beyond recognition. Curiously, schools that have such potential as interpreters of change and storehouses of creativity have for the most part stopped in their tracks. In the face of this change, schools seem stuck in the structures and approaches of the 1950s. Where has the much vaunted creativity revolution gone? The rhetorical and academic discussions for creativity in education have shifted substantially in the last five years. Several key international initiatives have brought the profile for creativity in primary, secondary and tertiary education to the fore. While there has been a significant shift in the discussion of creativity internationally, this has not always filtered into the classroom, not even the drama classroom. As Robinson argues, schools often extol the virtues of creativity but are organized against any possibility of it actually emerging: '. . . if the government were to design an education system to inhibit creativity, it could hardly do better . . . Governments throughout the world emphasize the importance of creativity, but often what they do in education suppresses it' (2001, p. 41). In the face of rapid and unrelenting change, schools are changing but perhaps not fast enough to ensure their survival as institutions that enjoy widespread community confidence.

Schools are changing . . . but perhaps not fast enough

There is little doubt that the traditional roles of classroom interaction are challenged by the introduction of technology throughout the history of education (Carroll, Anderson and Cameron, 2006). The dissemination of online technologies into the home and the classroom have provided great challenges for those Prensky (2001) calls 'digital immigrant' educators striving to make pedagogy and technology complement each other.

Drama teachers, like other performing arts educators, perhaps feel this most keenly. Though teachers are familiar with technology through theatrical technology (light and sound), the emerging technologies challenge the basis of drama education experience – the live body in a theatrical space. This challenge has provided some questions for those interested in drama education.

- How have drama's aesthetic characteristics been changed by new technologies and what is the emerging practice that is born of the marriage of the 'live' and the 'virtual'?
- How has this changed the relationship between students and teachers, if at all?
- How has the nature of drama education as a theoretical construct evolved because of this approach?

The ideas that emerge from these questions should assist us in understanding the way forward.

Students are changing

The debate about if and how young people are changing is raging among neurophysiologists, educators and psychologists. Mostly the discussion focuses on the idea that young people think differently because the vital neurological connections that are created during adolescence are being changed by the ways they interact with technology. Owston (2009, p. 270) reports that young people are spending as much time per day immersed in technologies through screens, mp3 players and the like as most people spend at work (6.5 hours). Marc Prensky (among others) claims that most of the current teaching workforce are digital immigrants who have learnt the languages and customs of the digital world rather than being born into them. Their students, digital natives by contrast, have been born into this new world and of course it is not new to them; they can speak digital languages and bridge the digital divides. Prensky argued that understanding brain plasticity was at the centre of these changes and there was recognition of this change, but '. . . the bulk of today's tradition-bound educational establishment seem in no hurry to follow their lead [digital natives]. Yet these educators know *something* is wrong, because they are not reaching their Digital Native students as well as they reached students in the past. So they face an important choice' (2001, p. 3).

Prensky's position has been criticized (Buckingham, 2008) but he is just the latest in a long line of educators who criticizes the schooling system's response to change and the challenges of Information and Communications Technologies (ICT) in particular. Buckingham argues (2008):

This relentlessly optimistic view inevitably ignores many of the downsides of these technologies – the undemocratic tendencies of many online 'communities', the limited nature of much so-called

> digital learning and the grinding tedium of much technologically driven work. It also tends to romanticize young people, offering a wholly positive view of their critical intelligence and social responsibility . . . (2008, p. 15)

This critique presents a view of learning that does not romanticize students or the technologies they use. Buckingham is the latest in a tradition of researchers and academics to advise caution in the face of the onslaught of technological change. A review of the digital natives debate (Bennett, Maton and Kervin, 2008) argues that there has been a kind of 'academic moral panic' that lacks rigorous evidence (p. 783). Australian research has found first-year university students have varying relationships with technology. This variability highlights the fundamental problem of assuming universal trends when designing curricula and learning approaches. As the researchers comment: 'When one moves beyond entrenched technologies and tools (for example, computers, mobile phones, email), the patterns of access to, use of and preference for a range of other technologies show considerable variation' (Churchward, Gray, Judd, Kennedy and Krause, 2008, p. 117).

Discussions about the place of technology in the classroom have swung from those who suggest that technology will be the end of cultural identity (Postman, 1993) to others who see technology in messianic terms (Negroponte, 1995). This tension has also permeated the discussions that relate to ICT in education naturally enough. Goodyear (2000) argues that ICT is beginning to deal with the emergent realities of the classroom. He argues that the decline of the compliant learner, a more user centred educational technology and evolving educational design, now offers more pedagogically appropriate ways of designing and utilizing ICT in learning environments. While Goodyear may have a point, there are still deep curriculum-specific issues with the application of technology to learning. In the face of this, students are engaging with technology as digital natives (Prensky, 2001) and bringing that experience to the classroom. The digital immigrants in this encounter (the teachers) are often left wondering how they might respond to this challenge where the body has been made marginal and role is engendered and rendered potentially redundant through the online world.

At the risk of rehearsing the arguments between Prensky and others over generalizing the attributes of any particular generation, there is a particular feature of this current generation of learners that absolutely delineates them from their predecessors. They have an unprecedented access to the tools of creation through the technologies available to them. That is not to say they know how to use these tools. This surely is one of the aspirations of modern education: to provide universal access to the tools of citizenship and creativity (including the arts) so that all may have access to the social capital on offer. Economic and social divides mean this aspiration often goes unfulfilled, but it is an underlying motivation for many educators nonetheless. If this is the case, then teachers have the responsibility to access, or in some cases demand, equal access to the tools of creativity for their students. As Stephen Heppel says:

> Computers are everyday tools for us all, seen or unseen, but their value in learning is as tools for creativity and learning rather than as machines to deliver the curriculum. These tools, in our children's

hands, are forever pushing the envelope of expertize that previous technologies excluded them from . . . . Little of this was easily achieved in the school classroom ten years ago. (Heppel, 2007)

Drama education has not been immune to these rapid curriculum changes. Drama sits in a unique place in the curriculum at the intersection between intellectual, creative and embodied education.

Drama teaching in the twenty-first century

In the face of this change, drama teachers have at their disposal an enormously powerful pedagogy that has the potential for transforming young people. It may first be wise to outline the ways drama is manifested in the curriculum. According to O'Toole and O'Mara (2007, p. 204), there are four 'paradigms of purpose' or if you like reasons for teaching drama.

They are:

1. Cognitive/procedural – gaining knowledge and skills in drama
2. Expressive/developmental – growing through drama
3. Social/pedagogical – learning through drama
4. Functional – learning what people do in drama

This is a useful way to analyse the reasons for teaching drama. Perhaps most teachers are doing all of the above in roughly equal measure. Your understanding of these paradigms will tell you a great deal about the teacher you are and the teacher you will be. Incidentally they also indicate how drama education has developed, but that is another story that we shall revisit later in the book.

Preparing generation next for the challenges of the next millennium

Since the turn of the last century, there has been renewed interest in the ways young people might be prepared for the demands of the new/creative economies through arts education. The landmark *Champions of Change* (Fiske, 1999) research allowed arts educators to speak with one voice about the documented evidence for the efficacy of the arts in the lives of young people. As O'Toole and O'Mara (2007, p. 204) argue, the terms creativity, communication, collaboration and teamwork, which are 'core business' in drama teaching, have been appropriated by those in the commercial sector and as a result, have been prominent in public discourses. As society, work and the world generally change from an individualistic approach that still dominates our schooling (think of children doing silent individual work which is the mainstay of many subjects), we are faced with a society that is profoundly disconnecting with the needs of students. Drama education and arts education generally is a pedagogy with a heritage that has the potential to modernize schooling.

Before we get carried away with overblown rhetorical discussion about the power of drama education, I would like to outline in a similar manner to the general principles above, what in my view constitutes drama teaching and how it is changing in response to this generation of learners and teachers. Here (in no particular order) are five principles that underpin my approach to the teaching of drama and permeate this book as guiding principles.

1. Drama teaching is transformative

There has been a tendency among some in drama education to claim that what we do in the classroom is a cure-all for those things that currently ail us. Recently Jonothan Neelands explored the concept of the miraculous in drama teaching to try and understand this approach born of advocacy and hope. He explains:

> I use the term 'miracles' here to describe accounts of events which claim some profound and new change in a student. Such miracles can also function as symbols of hope and faith within the struggles of everyday classroom life. They can also be treated as 'holy' and 'scriptural' in their cultural usages. Miracles can and do happen. These localized stories of hope are echoed sometimes in the claims of researchers and others in the field whose hero narratives include evangelized reports of personal victories in making miracles happen against all odds. These stories, embedded in the liberal humanist tradition, become the proof of drama's efficacy in resolving a range of 'problems' which might include various forms of student dysfunctionality or student resistance to the orthodoxy of the school's curriculum plan and practices. (2004, p. 47)

This approach also arises out of a general assumption that the arts is necessarily a good thing and that all of us are somehow enriched by being part of them. Jon Carey argues in his book *What Good Are the Arts?* that the notion that the arts are good for us goes back to Aristotle's times (2006, p. 96). While there may be some truth in this, we must now articulate for those who control the gates, the purse strings and the curriculum why the arts is needed and what in particular drama education does to support the academic, social and emotional growth of young people. Almost without exception, every teacher of maths, science, woodwork and so on believes inherently of the importance of their subject within the curriculum; drama teachers and researchers also need to be specific about which parts of their pedagogy are transformative and what specifically is being transformed.

2. Drama teaching is aesthetic education

I was once in a meeting with an international theatre director at a very well known theatre company discussing their new education program. At one point, the theatre director leant across the table and said to me in a stage whisper 'you know, what we do here in the theatre, is not the same as what happens in the school curriculum for drama'. At the time I thought that she had uncovered a large deficiency in the way we teach drama in schools. With the benefit of experience, I realize that she had identified a central paradox of the work drama teachers do in schools. In my view, we do not and cannot mirror exactly what happens in professional theatre. The theatre and the drama classroom – while inter-related – are not the same thing and do not and should not be looking for the same out-comes. Schools are obviously different in their aims and circumstances from theatres are and can be. While drama teachers know how important their subject is, there are a host of others in a school arguing for the centrality of their area of study as well. The school is sometimes a marketplace with many ideas, approaches and philosophies vying for the students' attention.

Drama education, like music education and visual arts education, draws centrally from the aesthetics of the art form while not actually being the same as theatre. The processes and approaches are not the same, nor should they be. This often leads to prominent theatre practitioners suggesting that there is no relationship between the theatre and education so much so that Howard Barker argued in *Arguments for a Theatre* that '. . . theatre is the last place you would go to "learn" something' (1997, p. 137). There is however a rich tradition of the aesthetics and content of theatrical innovation being integrated into classroom drama practice (See Chapter Three, A History of Drama Education) into classroom settings. As Helen Nicholson argues:

> Crucially, because theatre that seeks to engage young people looks to the future, it often articu-lates a vision of social change and educational aspirations. Contemporary practitioners in the field are indebted, therefore to a rich tradition of theatrical experimentation that was fuelled by political discussion, and, sometimes, both marred and enriched by dispute and divisions. (2009, p. 12)

Nicholson's summation articulates the relationship elegantly. There is a strong relationship between effective theatre and effective education that relates directly to shared imaginings. The mistake some then make is to suppose they are somehow the same thing. They are not, and nor should they ever be, in my view.

Drama teaching: Making and appreciating

At the centre of effective teaching in the arts is an interdependent relationship between making and appreciating. Depending on your context, this might be called forming and responding, generating and realizing or constructing and deconstructing. This kind of arts education hands the tools of creation (derived largely in drama from a theatre aesthetic) directly to the student. This 'handing over' is crucial (Anderson, Cameron and Carroll, 2006, p. xiii). Knowledge about theatre or drama should not be left to the adults but shared freely with young people. This generation of students have more ready access to knowledge through the networked digital world than any generation before them, but experience-based knowledge can still be difficult to access for most young people. If making is central to an arts curriculum, it will engage students as artists (albeit fledgling) and immerse them in the richness of the aesthetic. This provides students with access to the tools of creation and allows them to be involved in learning beyond aesthetic literacy to be creators within the art form. This is real multi-literacy.

Students who can understand the language, codes and craft of the creative process while simultaneously being involved in the process of creation are able to create and analyse, with both processes feeding into each other. This interaction is crucial. To have making without appreciation could potentially see the drama classroom descend into a place where everything is acceptable and not much learning occurs. Drama educators such as Peter Slade (1958) proposed this kind of approach in response, it must be said, to the autocratic transmissive classrooms that he experienced. While there is no doubt that there is integrity in young people's work that must be nurtured and appreciated, it must also be supported by promoting depth of understanding of the aesthetics of drama.

At the other end of the spectrum has been the tendency to appreciate the art form without giving attention to student's experience of making in that art form. John O'Toole et al. (2009) describes English classrooms where many teachers remain ambivalent to the making processes involved in drama while clinging closely to the primacy of 'the word' (p. 49). He argues that for some English teachers, the concept of a classroom as a '. . . public performance space, where dialogue happens' is '. . . entirely foreign and quite threatening'. Again in this situation, students are being denied access to the power of the aesthetic. This situation is not only disappointing because of the lost opportunities; perhaps more disturbingly, it leaves students disliking drama because they have only glimpsed the experience as an audience and not as theatre makers. Perhaps the worst case of this has emerged from that noxious (but seemingly ineradicable) approach of reading Shakespeare 'around the room'. This approach is so damaging because all the dramatic tension, characterization and poetry of the language is stripped out and students are left with poorly presented language, devoid of any physicality that is inexplicable to most present (including the teacher on many occasions).

A relationship in learning between making and appreciating lays the foundations for effective and dynamic arts experiences in the classroom. For teachers of drama, the concepts of aesthetic understanding and aesthetic control discussed later are the bases of effective drama education.

3. Drama teaching is research informed

The health of drama education in the early twenty-first century can be seen in the growth and maintenance of key research structures in the field. The very existence of several journals including *Research in Drama Education*, *Applied Theatre Researcher*, *NJ, The National Journal of Drama, Australia* and journals with a broader agenda in Arts education such as *Arts Education Policy Review* and *Journal of Aesthetic Education* have been crucial to the ongoing strength of the area. The establishment and ongoing success of IDEA, the International Drama, Theatre and Education Association and its International congresses, the ongoing success of the International Drama in Education Research Institute (IDIERI) and their triennial conference; and numerous national and local research conferences and publications attest to the strength of the area. Taken together, these institutions have created infrastructure for drama education research and practice. There are now professors of drama education in several countries, supervising and coordinating large externally funded research projects relating to drama education and applied theatre, and laying the foundations for the next generation of researchers into our field.

In arts education, landmark studies including Creative Partnerships (Thomson and Sanders, 2010), Champions of Change (Fiske, 1999), Reviewing Education and the Arts Project (REAP) (Hetland and Winner, 2001), Critical Links (Deasy, 2004) and the Evaluation of School-based Arts Education Programmes in Australian Schools (ACER, 2004) have provided a base for the recent burgeoning of further externally funded arts education research. Drama educators who work with schools have been funded to explore how for example drama can combat bullying and manage conflict in schools (O'Toole et al., 2005). Large funded research studies have explored young people's preferences in the theatre through the TheatreSpace program (Australian Research Council, 2007–2011. For more information on this study go to www.theatrespace.org.au/), how marginalized students are supported through drama and the arts (Donellan and O'Brien, 2008) and how drama and other art forms motivate and engage students in learning across the curriculum. Drama education has an active and thriving research community that is situated for the most part in classroom research. The next principle touches on the sometimes fractious history of drama education.

4. Drama teaching is process and product

The history of drama education has been driven in some places by feuds over how close education should be to the actual practices of theatre. This debate is often referred to as the process versus product debate. My view on this closely aligns to O'Toole and O'Mara's characterization of drama in the 'unifying paradigm' (2007, p. 213). They argue that this approach values a tripartite learning framework often called making, performing and appreciating. Whatever the terms used, this approach identifies the understanding of the art form and the making of the art form as central to the learning. This position makes redundant the ultimately useless and fruitless discussions around process versus product. Drama in schools does not necessarily look like professional theatre (and neither should it). Theatre is the aesthetic *wellspring* that drama educators need to constantly draw from so that the dynamism and innovation apparent within the art form can be interpreted and communicated through teaching and learning. At its heart drama education is providing access to an aesthetic way of knowing that goes beyond the mind/body or process/product dichotomies. Rather the strength of drama learning is that it is 'joined up' pedagogy that allows young people to engage more of themselves in a potentially deeper learning experience.

5. Drama education is the productive pedagogy

Drama learning is a snug fit within the 'productive pedagogies', 'New Basics' or 'Quality Teaching' movement. Emerging originally from American research into 'authentic pedagogies' (Newman, 1996) was the Queensland School Reform Longitudinal Survey (QSRLS, 2001) that has provided the most recent impetus for this approach. This research argued for four dimensions of classroom practice that particularly supported learning of students that had been marginalized by traditional schooling (Hayes et al., 2006, p. 8). The dimensions they uncovered were:

- Intellectual quality
- Connectedness
- Supportive classroom environment
- Working with and valuing difference

There are strong claims that drama is a tight fit with the productive pedagogies model (O'Toole, 2002; Martello, 2004). John O'Toole recognized what many drama teachers already implicitly understand, 'That . . . drama in schools can amply fulfil all twenty requirements of the Productive Pedagogies, as a Productive Pedagogy singular. Could drama be the New Basic? Based on children's play it is certainly the oldest of Old Basics' (2002, p. 52). Notwithstanding the obvious match between drama education pedagogy and productive pedagogies, there has been little linkage between the two by those in the productive pedagogies or new basics movement. As O'Toole et al. (2009, p. 107) argue, drama figures 'nowhere' in the examples or the substance of the professional development materials in the area.

Conclusions

There is a compelling case to be argued that drama, one of the oldest art forms is uniquely placed to meet the demands of young people and their education in the twenty-first century. The move to a more digital society has ironically meant that liveness, immediacy and negotiation of relationships are growing in importance in the education of young people. Schools have changed little to meet many of the changes occurring rapidly in society, but drama could be the catalyst to make these changes happen in many curriculum contexts.

Drama has the capacity to meet those emerging needs, but also to connect young people with a growing understanding of how they might act morally, ethically, sustainably and democratically in an ever-changing world. The next chapter discusses the challenges that a new generation of learners presents.

2 The Challenge of Generation Next

I worked for a while as a bureaucrat within a large education administration. My official title was 'drama consultant', but much of my time was taken up attempting to translate departmental or government directives into drama education pedagogy. Sometimes this was simple; for instance, finding drama education examples that fit with productive pedagogies. On other occasions it was more difficult, for example, finding ways we can use spreadsheets in the drama classrooms. This last example came about when the Department of Education decided it needed to respond to the rapid rise in computer-based technology in the community. Even though they were ten years late and we at this stage had no computers to write anything on, we still needed to produce something. The problem with what we had to produce was that it misunderstood what technology is for in the arts. Rather than finding a piece of technology (such as spreadsheets), we should have recognized then that digital technology in the arts is a creativity tool, rather than a machine for facts or rows of numbers. I often wonder how much richer our drama classrooms could have been if we had recognized that the potential for creativity lies where it always did, in the mind and bodies of those in the classroom, rather than the machines. The machines, software and programs are tools of creation just like the old technologies, pens, paper, lights and so on. So as Jaron Lanier argues, the web should not only be seen as a repository of facts but a place to make collaborative creativity thrive.

What we see with interactive media like the Web is not only the end result of the creative process, but the creative process itself, set down for all people to see and to share. This is extraordinarily exciting. (Jaron Lanier, 1998)

In a book about drama education with a future focus, we must consider critically the intersections and tensions between drama and technology. While technology is not the only challenge or opportunity that faces us, it is one that deserves some reflection. This chapter argues that drama is one of the best sites in the curriculum to engage students in creativity with digital technology. The drama classroom has the potential not only to teach the 'how', but also the implications of their creation on seen and unseen audiences, whether this creativity is mediated through technology such as digital film or through staging (which is a mediation and technology as well). This chapter explores how discourses around creativity, technology and learning might be brought to fruition in learning and teaching in drama. Let's start with a discussion of the generation of students that faces us in our classrooms every day.

A new generation of learners?

When Douglas Coupland (1992) invented the phrase Generation X to describe his generation, he began the inextricable link between a demographic group and the technology that permeates and converges with their lives. While the baby boomers were named because of a demographic dynamic, each generation from Generation X down has been considered in terms of the technology they live with. To Generation X technology is far more integrated in their lives than their parents. This is far more so for the generation Y's who are growing up with Ipods, Ipads, Playstation Portables and media on demand as if it has always existed. This technology is not strange to them like their predecessors because it is like the radio and television to the previous generations. In Prensky's terms, the current generation in schools are natives of the technology whereas the Baby Boomer Generation, Generation X and all in between are immigrants to this place where technology is pervasive. Kathryn Montgomery (2007, p. 2) agrees: 'Never before has a generation been so defined in the public mind by its relationship to technology. Pollsters, market researchers, and journalists closely track their every move, inventing a gaggle of catchy buzz words to describe them . . .'

As a digital immigrant Gen X educator, it still strikes me as odd that places of learning including schools and universities are even now approaching technology as a novelty commodity worthy of reverence and/or fear. As schooling systems run largely by digital immigrant administrators still control the levers (rather than switches or the remotes), many students are taught in the same teaching spaces with much the same transmissive pedagogies. Even attempts at updating teaching technologies such as use of electronic whiteboards reinforce 'chalk and talk' approaches to teaching. The teacher writes or points to a website and the students dutifully respond with attention. More realistically, they SMS or Facebook their friends as they become less engaged in that learning and more engaged in other technologies. The typical response of course is to ban the distractions and demand student attention to an outmoded pedagogical methodology. There are uses for the electronic white-board like any technology, but it is not a panacea for updating learning. A total reorientation is required in the way we teach drama to meet this generation of learners at their point of need: high levels of familiarity (and ownership) of technology (Carroll, Anderson and Cameron, 2006) and often low levels of aesthetic control and critical engagement.

Digital Natives in the drama classroom

Coupland is not the only author to attempt to categorize the generations that have their identity linked with digital technologies. According to Douglas Rushkoff (2005), this generation are active participants in the development and dissemination of digital materials for all sorts of reasons and in many places. These digital natives (Prensky, 2001) face none of the barriers to understanding and comprehension of the new world that the digital immigrants who have come before them did. Their use of technology is an informed use where the techno-fear of the previous generations seems quaint to the digital natives of today. This is the generation that has grown up with dynamic and rapid video editing, mass media, the Internet and video games machines. The screen is not an unwanted intrusion; it is a pervasive and integral facet of their lives.

Young people are seeking out technologies that will enhance their lifestyles. Research by Carroll and Peck (2002, np) suggested young people appropriate technology to '. . . add value to their lifestyles, satisfy their social and leisure needs and reinforce their group identity'. Additionally they found that technology was influenced heavily by the situation of use. These findings raise some significant challenges for those examining the place of technology in education. If our students are appropriating technology as part of their lifestyles, how can we make the technology of the drama classroom part of their learning? How can the mp3, digital video and the Playstation be used to greater effect in the drama classroom? And is the drama classroom suited and/or ready for the challenge of technology?

About educational technology

Digital technology is rather like a pendulum in the public imagination. The moral panics often enacted with melodramatic flair by schooling systems banning this or blocking that often provides real barriers. Jensen (2007, p. 20) reports several instances of restrictive system behaviour that hobbles and impairs the use of technology. The other extreme has been an unfortunate tendency of educators to follow with some short-sightedness the claims made by the computer industry about technology. Predictably, every new product will provide 'solutions' to an educator's 'problem'. Recently many wealthy countries have promised computers for each school student. Another version of this policy in developing countries can be seen in the L4L programme putting laptops in the hands of children in poorer countries. Again the computer industry is setting the agenda and not the educators. Michael Apple warned against this tendency more than two decades ago. He said, '. . . we are in the midst of one of those many educational bandwagons that governments, industry, and others like to ride. This wagon is pulled in the direction of a technological workplace, and carries a heavy load of computers as its cargo' (1991, p. 42).

The drama classroom of the future (and for some students the present) might use these laptops as a tool for the realization of student imaginations and creativity through scripts, screenplays, films and the like. To achieve this, students who are already immersed in this technology need to understand how to control it and how to realize a creative vision using these new highly powered tools. This provision of technology to the already reasonably well connected is only the beginning of the task. The most pressing need is to provide the necessary learning opportunities for this kind of technology to be used as a tool of creation in the classroom.

Generation Next

The society's approach to this generation has been at best ambivalent and at worst fearful. As Kathryn Montgomery observes:

> In our collective effort to make sense of this new generation, the public discourse often has been contradictory, reflecting an ambivalent attitude toward both youth and technology. As our children have ventured fearlessly into cyberspace, seizing upon all manner of digital gismos and gadgets, the public has responded with a mix of wonder, fear, and perplexity. (2007, p. 2)

For the most part, the current generation of students have virtually unfettered access to the means and distribution of digital production. Even children in third world countries now have access to mobile telephony, which albeit restricted and relatively low tech, still has the potential for creative production and distribution (camera and data transfer) (Carroll, Anderson and Cameron, 2006). As Montgomery says (2007, p. 2): 'As active creators of a new digital culture, these youth are developing their own Websites, diaries, and blogs; launching their own online enterprises; and forging a new set of cultural practices'. While Generation Next has leapt ahead, society in general and schooling in particular has often lagged, struggling to make pedagogical sense of these new tools of digital creation.

The danger here is for schooling systems to put the technology cart (or the 'wagon' as Michael Apple calls it) in front of the learning horse. Providing students access to technology, while essential, is only the first part of the process. Without tailoring technology to meet the needs of the drama classroom (or any other classroom), the technology is virtually and actually redundant.

A more effective approach to learning technologies for the drama classroom employs as Jaron Lanier rather prophetically put it more than a decade ago (1998) a '. . . balanced attitude towards technology and aesthetics, in which you neither shy away from nor worship technology, but enjoy the rush of being able to create entirely new things with it . . .' Technology is not a choice any longer for students in the drama classroom. It is an integral part of their lives. The question is: how can we harness the technology to meet the needs of our students and reinvigorate our pedagogy to embrace the creative potential of this generation of learners?

Generation Next learners

As we discussed in Chapter One, there is now compelling (albeit contested) new advice from the research that this generation learns differently from their predecessors. This generation's exposure to pervasive and persistent technologies means that they are less linear in their approach to learning. Mabrito and Medley (2008) argue: '. . . N-Gen [Generation next] students are literally wired differently from previous generations, their brains shaped by a lifelong immersion in virtual spaces. Repeated and prolonged exposure to the digital world may mean that N-Gen students process and interact with information in a fundamentally different way from those who did not grow up in this environment'.

In addition to this generation learning differently they have a ubiquitous and often intrusive media pushing messages through their screens at a bewildering rate. According to the Kaiser institute this generation has more exposure to media than any other generation and it is delivered on far more platforms (phones, Ipods and handheld games platforms). They argue that this exposure means that children come to formal schooling more exposed to the screen than any other form of literacy. According to an American study released in 2010 'Over the past five years [2005–2010], young people have increased the amount of time they spend consuming media by an hour and seventeen minutes daily, from 6:21 to 7:38—almost the amount of time most adults spend at work each day, except that young people use media seven days a week instead of five' (Kaiser Family Foundation, 2010, p. 2).

There are some valid concerns in this rate of screen media consumption including potential lessening of physical activity and exposure to inappropriate content. There is an opportunity here to use all this media exposure (which is not the same as aesthetic understanding or aesthetic control) to develop critical readings of the eight and a half hours of media messages they receive on a daily basis (Kaiser Family Foundation, 2006, p. 57). This large number is attributed to young people consuming multiple media at the same time, for example, radio, computer, television and so on. This is a form of multiple synchronous viewing. This ultimately helps students make their own decisions about the media they watch and the media that they produce by giving them access to the tools of creation and an ability to be critical.

Providing Generation Next with the tools of creation

A central precept of arts education has been the provision of the tools of aesthetic creation. In drama education this is sometimes manifest in students' informed creation of their own dramatic work through the improvization and playbuilding process. As Anderson and Jefferson (2009) argue in arts education, appreciation is only fully possible when it is integrated with making processes. In this model of learning, simply appreciating theatre (for instance) is not sufficient. It is also necessary to be involved in the creation process. As Goldman, Booker and McDermott (2007) argue, digital technologies have the potential to be a transformative power for this generation of young people, not just as producers or consumers, but as creators; 'Learning with increased participation, engagement, commitment, and action changes both the youth themselves and the vision of the adults who work with them . . . scaffolding ways for youth to participate, working with them, and eventually enabling power shifts that allow youth to define participation on their own terms' (2007, p. 202).

While access is more or less a given in Western societies (Carroll, Anderson and Cameron, 2006) through families and schools, access is only really the first step on a much longer and more complex journey. Teachers' roles are changing, but many of the traditional skills and understanding of drama teaching remain in place.

Teaching Generation Next in the drama classroom

The role of the teacher in this new pedagogical landscape is similar to the role that the teacher has always taken. I am aware teachers take on myriad roles including welfare, administration and so on. Teachers deepen the knowledge, skills and understanding that students already have, and extend deepen and enrich them. Although they may have unprecedented access to technology, students do not necessarily know how to create an effective script or craft an engaging character on stage. The craft that is the foundation of the creative process still needs to be taught to allow young people to deepen their understanding of the dramatic form. Even though Generation Next is saturated in media (Kaiser Family Foundation, 2010), they are not necessarily more equipped to create or appreciate the aesthetics of drama and theatre. So while the technology may be new(ish), the teacher's job is the same – to deepen and extend the understanding of their students.

Implications for Generation Next

To extend this discussion of Generation Next in the drama classroom I have identified some of the implications for the learners we now face. These are tentative and speculative and as such I have not labelled them 'principles', but they could be a useful framework for drama educators to begin the redesign and rethinking process required to meet the learning needs of these students.

Implication 1: learning is socially mediated
The standard popular vision of this generation is that they are isolated – immersed in their own technology as their social relationships degrade. While this view may get some airplay

in the popular media, the reality is predictably a little more complex. There is emerging evidence that there is more collaborative and networked learning emerging as a result of the way these young people learn and their access to social media. Gee argues that 'traditional' classrooms reward 'individual knowledge' rather than allowing student collaboration (2007, p. 103). The exception to this is in the humanities classrooms (in particular drama and English) where since the time of Henry Caldwell Cook (1885–1939) at least (see next chapter), there has been a tradition of collaboration in the classroom.

Generation Next challenges those teaching drama curriculum to develop communities of practice (Lave and Wenger, 1991) that surpass the opportunities that already exist and take advantage of the new social relationships and networks being created by these students. While still embryonic, there are exciting possibilities emerging for collaborative authoring of texts that feature multiple media (Anderson, 2009; Hughes and McGeoch, 2009; Raphael, 2009) as students collaborate across tables and/or across nations. The prevalence of Twitter, Facebook and other social networking sites provide a glimpse of what might be possible when collaboration is allowed to flourish in the drama classroom.

Of course, there are difficulties with this approach. Collaborative learning requires different pedagogical approaches from teachers as they work to structure and restructure classrooms to meet the needs of the collaboration. An added level of opportunity (and perhaps difficulty) is presented when networked and collaborative technologies are thrown into the mix. Whatever the challenges, these new learners give the chance for the drama classroom to be transformed with new approaches to teacher-to-student, peer-to-peer and other emergent learning modes. The next challenge lies in teacher scaffolding and supporting student choices of appropriate technology for learning in the drama classroom.

Implication 2: learning is about controlling appropriate technologies, not just using them

As I have discussed earlier, there has been some 'shock and awe' surrounding new technologies that is not fully justified by its usefulness in learning. Giving students access to the tools of creation is only the beginning; the next crucial step is supporting students' growing control of appropriate technologies. Again, the teacher rather than being redundant, is central to the learning. Without the teacher actively managing the learning and collaboration of the classroom, the technologies that are potentially powerful can be expensive time-wasters. In this approach, scaffolding the learning choices for students is the key. To illustrate what I mean here, let us think about the way that film is currently taught in the drama classroom and what potential for teaching it might have.

In any of the modern standard computer-based editing packages that now come with many home PCs, there is a vast array of effects that can be applied to the editing process. These can, if introduced too early to the learning, diminish student's understanding of the editing process. When teaching students this skill, their grasp of editing for meaning is enhanced if they focus on the narrative they are trying to convey rather than the bewildering variety of edit approaches and effects available to them. In this simple example, the teacher has a role in structuring the learning and assisting students to make informed aesthetic choices. This learning scaffolding highlights the importance of the teacher's role in the selection and deployment of the most appropriate technologies. Rather than being dazzled by the gadgetry and overwhelmed by this generation's access to the technology, the teacher must provide learning scope and sequence in the same way teachers always have. This new approach to drama learning will also have implications for the physical learning spaces as well.

Implication 3: learning spaces must change

One of the features of Generation Next learning is that interactivity is prized (Mabrito and Medley, 2008). This means that the way we design our virtual and physical spaces borrow from the pedagogic interactivity of Caldwell-Cook's workshop and the virtual interactivity that is so engaging on the web for so many young people. Perhaps this means that we should reconceptualize learning as taking place not completely in the virtual world or the physical classroom space, but in a mixture of both. Mabrito and Medley (2008) argue that this mixed approach that mirrors the social interactivity, discussed earlier, (social constructivism) more closely resembles the social interactivity Generation Next (or the N-Gen, as they call them) has online: 'A pedagogy grounded in principles of social constructivism recognizes many of the approaches to learning that N-Gen students may adopt in creating their texts outside of the classroom. These principles include the construction of meaning through shared social experiences (Vygotsky, 1978) that are facilitated through dialogue and interaction among members of a community' (Wenger, 1998).

The pedagogic implications here are reasonably straightforward: many members of Generation Next learn by doing; by creating. Perhaps this is no different to the generation that preceded them, but their access and immersion in these technologies has made the creative process more accessible. The runaway popularity of sites such as YouTube is evidence for this creativity culture. Young people create films often on their mobile phones and then upload them to websites such as YouTube that affords them a global audience. The popularity of their work then becomes an additional platform for interactivity as others post video responses or blog about their work. The major pitfall in this approach is lack of aesthetic quality. While the access is available, the ability to shape creative work is not as strong. A casual meander through YouTube will demonstrate lack of attention to the art form of film-making. The drama teacher's role is to use this virtual space to create a pedagogic space by adding to it the scaffolding required for a rich learning experience. Having achieved that, the learning is there for all to see and interact with.

Implication 4: new media should be taught alongside traditional literature in the classroom

The place of traditional texts is not diminished in the drama classroom of the future. On the contrary, if we expect our students to create work of aesthetic quality, it is essential that they are able to appreciate the features of engaging plays and other dramatic texts (such as films, radio plays and so on).

In addition to classical texts, Generation Next study the texts they encounter in their everyday lives. 'These texts often serve to present the author to the digital world and may be collaboratively composed and edited; they are frequently multimodal, integrating words, graphics, sound, and video' (Mabrito and Medley, 2008). These texts present fresh challenges for drama teachers. How is work created collaboratively assessed? What criteria can be attached to works that include elements of design, music, and so on? We already have well known approaches for assessing collaborative work that predate the current generation (Anderson and Manuel, 2008). The discussion on multiliteracies also equips us to cope with multimodal texts. Mabrito and Medley argue that these new texts (2008) provide significant issues for teachers. If teachers:

> . . . perceive linear, print-based texts as a benchmark, the N-Gen's texts may, at first glance, fall quite short. However, these digital texts do not necessarily lack style, coherence, or organization; they simply present meaning in ways unfamiliar to the instructor. For example, a collection of images on Flickr with authorial comments and tags certainly does not resemble the traditional essay, but the time spent on such a project, the motivation for undertaking it, and its ability to communicate meaning can certainly be equal to the investment and motivation required by the traditional essay . . . and the photos may actually provide more meaningful communication for their intended audience. (2008, p. 3)

Perhaps the challenge is to recognize the richness that already exists in drama pedagogy and adapt it to meet the needs of this generation of students. While not neglecting learning and assessment tasks (like the essay), there is a place for the appreciation and creation of texts that are founded in the principles of aesthetic quality and literacy even though they may be expressed in new forms.

Conclusions

This chapter has called for a reorientation of our approach to Generation Next. Drama teachers need to seriously consider the ramifications of excluding technology from learning and the detrimental effects this may have on our students' access to creativity. It is also worth stressing that technology is not value-free and that using it for its own sake rather than for the sake of our students is potentially damaging. In 1991, Michael Apple provided this warning about the motivations for integrating technology in the classroom:

> The new technology is here. It will not go away. Our task as educators is to make sure that when it enters the classroom it is there for politically, economically, and educationally wise reasons, not because powerful groups may be redefining our major educational goals in their own image. We should be very clear about whether or not the future it promises our students is real, not fictitious. (1991, p. 82)

Decades later the same challenges remain. The difference however is that technology has permeated almost all aspects of the lives of the young people we teach and drama, and pedagogy must respond dynamically and ethically or become irrelevant. This chapter is calling for two seemingly contradictory changes to the teaching of drama: a wholesale change and no change at all. The way we teach drama must shift radically to meet the needs of a new generation who have unprecedented access to the means of production and distribution of creative product. At the same time, however, we have within our current pedagogy the means to guide and support this creative process. While these students have unprecedented access, aesthetic control and critical understanding are not learnt by osmosis. It is still, as it ever was, the teacher's role to scaffold and support the learning. The challenge for those teaching Generation Next is to work with them collaboratively to engage them in a world that they recognize and help them learn about worlds beyond their experience that are strange and wonderful. In essence the challenge drama teachers face now is the challenge they have always faced.

Perhaps before we venture too far into the challenges that the future holds, it may be worth spending some time reflecting on the influences of the past in drama education that shape our present and potentially our future.

3 A History of Drama Education

Adventures in Durham

I was in Durham a few years ago for a National Drama conference. At this conference was a mix of people who all at once represented drama's past, present and future. Some of the pioneers were there, Dorothy Heathcote and Gavin Bolton. There were also drama teachers and drama education researchers from Iceland, New Zealand, Australia, Greece, Ireland, Turkey, Malaysia and South America. For me it was a good conference where the best of research and practice intermingled without a whiff of disdain for either. In short it was an international community of educators that appreciated each other. At the same conference, I participated in a workshop led by Dorothy Heathcote, heard Gavin Bolton discuss the history of the field and learnt about the growth of drama education in Iceland and Ireland. Two things strike me about this reflection. First, drama education is now an international movement whose scholars come from everywhere. This conference was in a way symbolic for me of the maturing of the field. The voices are now African, Australian, Irish, Norwegian, Asian and Brazilian rather than just British. My second reflection about this conference was how generously those with knowledge were ready to share their ideas. It has become a little taken-for-granted in the field, but my experience is that generosity of spirit is a standard feature of this community and the same was true as a drama teacher, a drama bureaucrat and a drama researcher. This chapter provides a brief overview of some of the key figures in drama education that I will revisit throughout this book. In the contest of ideas that has been present in drama education, the internationalization and generosity of the community are sometimes lost, but they are nonetheless part of the historical climate of our field.

Modern drama education has a short but lively history that has shaped curriculum throughout the world. This chapter introduces some of these philosophies and provides a discussion of how drama education's history has provided the philosophical grounding for those who currently teach the subject. It explores the history of process drama, the theatre arts movement, creative dramatics and the blended models that pervade many parts of the world. This chapter also contains a discussion of the important and complex relationship between drama education and theatre practice generally, and argues for the importance of understanding the history of drama education as the basis for each teacher's individual philosophical approach to the subject. The history of drama education matters because it shapes the pedagogies, traditions and practices we see in classrooms today. It is probably also worth declaring that this is a personal history – shaped by those who have influenced me the most in my teaching and research.

Tensions in drama education

The history of drama education revolves around two main tensions that to some extent are still debated today. They surround the polarization of drama process and product and approach that value aesthetic discipline above play and exploration. As with the other art forms taught in schools, drama addresses a duality in its practice (students learn about the art form itself, but also through the art form). On the one hand, like perhaps music, drama is heavily influenced by professional practice in the theatre. So students learn to 'act' and design and so on (Bolton, 1998, p. XVI). On the other hand, students develop ways of knowing through the process of drama learning. Heathcote argues in her 1984 lectures that: 'If you want to use drama you're basically looking at social behaviours. You're not looking at the private person in the private moment; you're looking at social behaviours' (Heathcote, 1984a, p. 4).

Social behaviours are one of the learning objectives of drama syllabuses that are not necessarily the mainstay of the professional theatre even though the theatre is by nature collaborative. This paradox reflects the major philosophical positions in drama education. Theatre Arts refers to the learning that directly relates to theatre and its functions and apart from those objectives has little to do with social knowing. This approach is espoused strongly by David Hornbrook[1] who argues that there is essentially no difference between what a child does in the classroom and what an actor does on stage (Hornbrook, 1989). Through his publications, he has provided a critical voice mainly of the drama in education movement pioneered by Dorothy Heathcote and Gavin Bolton. His approach values the traditions of the theatre over what he calls the 'mystification and dramatic midwifery' (1989) of Heathcote and Bolton's practice. This controversial critic has provided an important other voice in the development of drama education.

Drama or process drama has its genesis with practitioners such as Peter Slade, but is most powerfully practiced by Dorothy Heathcote (as shown in her video *Three Looms Waiting* [BBC, 1976]). It relies on the power of the processes within drama to teach what it is to be human. It also assists in the development of social skills and promotes understandings of the other.

Pre-Heathcotian pioneers[2]

Gavin Bolton's work has illuminated most of the important figures in the pre-Heathcote era. His work on the genesis of the movement, found in several publications, but most significantly *Acting in Classroom Drama* (Bolton, 1998) provides an articulate analysis of the 'pioneers' of drama education. As he is one of the major scholars in this area and at times the only voice, his work clearly reflects his philosophical and political position. His closeness to the figures he writes about such as Heathcote is one of Hornbrook's (1989) major criticisms and discussion of figures such as Heathcote's work should be reviewed with this in mind. He has during the course of his career, revised his view on the nature of the 'pioneers' (Bolton, 1998, p. XVIII). His writing in this area is examined here and juxtaposed with available literature that critiques or complements his view.

Harriet Finlay-Johnson

From the earliest days of drama education, the movement has been inextricably linked with progressive education. Harriet Finlay-Johnson's book of 1911 called The *Dramatic Method of Teaching* was brought to light by the then Chief Inspector of Schools, Edmund Holmes. His reputation as a 'progressive', conflated Finlay-Johnson and drama education in the same camp. The identification of drama education as progressive, even from its early days, is significant and may explain some of the struggles for acceptance of the subject in the mainstream curriculum and some of the subject's internal political struggles.

Finlay-Johnson introduced some key concepts that influence contemporary practice. She worked with the idea of the construction of a 'virtual world' where students could work through the metaphor of a game. The game analogy is an important part of a drama teacher's language. Finlay-Johnson used the terms 'game' and 'drama' (Bolton, 1998, p. 22) interchangeably and this seems reasonable given that she was working with younger students. Bolton argues that the game introduces the idea of another schooling culture with different rules. That idea was borne out by Finlay-Johnson's description of her own classroom environment that included collaborative learning and teacher facilitation rather than the rote learning model that was predominant during the pre-war years. Finlay-Johnson was the first to practice and then theorize about drama education. She touched on many themes and tensions in her work that are important issues for drama teachers today.

Henry Caldwell Cook

Henry Caldwell Cook was a contemporary of Finlay-Johnson and introduced several concepts that continue to resonate. Again as Bolton (1998, p. 27) suggests, the link with progressivism was the key to the development of his concepts of dramatization. What Caldwell Cook brings to the field however is the discussion and examination of play and its links with drama education. In his book *Play Way; An Essay in Educational Method* (1917), he provides a discussion of how teachers might guide students through learning by facilitating their use of play and through collaboration. His methods encouraged using 'free play' to begin, followed by structured playbuilding that borrowed from the classics. The link between play and drama emerged with the pioneers and endures as a research theme today. Roslyn Arnold for instance argues that drama '. . . reactivates the pleasurable (or difficult) experiences of exploration, mastery and social interaction found in early childhood play' (1994, p. 17).

In the *Play Way; An Essay in Educational Method* (1917), he outlines nine advisory notes that describe the process of development. The ideas here value collaboration and process and refer only briefly to product. His last point illustrates the value he places on the product 'with older children there is value in sharing the work with an audience' (Caldwell Cook, 1917).

The tension between a regimented classroom practice and the development of a more exploratory approach (most typically seen in Peter Slade's work) formed the basis of an argument about the place of improvisation in the classroom. The debate continues, if on a slightly broader scale, focused on the development of self-devised versus scripted work in the classroom. This concern however does not insist on the removal of improvisation, but rather that it might be more closely related to the script, and by implication, the theatre. Thus, even though the argument over the place of improvisation in teaching drama first occurred several decades ago, the issues remain relevant and contentious. The place of improvisation and play also provided the fuel for debate in the drama education movement for the next three decades and beyond.

Peter Slade

Peter Slade commented in a radio interview in 1948 (cited in Bolton, 1998, p. 120) that 'these days it seems that Drama is almost in the air'. According to Bolton, his perception was correct. In the United Kingdom, there were conferences, publications and the Ministry of Education commissioned a report into drama education that brought recognition by 1951. It said of drama in the curriculum that '. . . drama can now be regarded as an established and worthwhile part of school life' (Hornbrook, 1989, p. 10). Peter Slade had involvement in many of these activities. His approach to drama education as outlined in *An Introduction to Child Drama* (Slade, 1958) sat well within the progressivism of the day. Hornbrook comments that *Child Drama* (Hornbrook, 1989, p. 10) and its follow-up came to inform the practice of a newly created generation of drama teachers.

Child Drama as a book and as a theory valued the child's drama as an art in itself that needed to be lovingly nurtured. Slade also stressed that the child's work should not be judged by adult standards. His ideas develop the work on play that others, most notably Caldwell Cook espoused in their work. Slade's work however developed and elevated the idea. Slade saw drama as 'the art of living'. His understanding of drama was all pervasive. Bolton suggests (1998, p. 121) that he never justified his broad usage of drama, but simply pointed to it as a phenomenon. Slade feels that drama is at the centre of life, education and all the arts. This claim was sure to bring some resistance. One of the critiques comes from David Hornbrook who writes: 'If the teacher's relationship with Child Drama was vitally non-critical, then how was it possible to know what educational aims were being realized'? (Hornbrook, 1989, p. 10). This valid concern of Hornbrook's raised two major issues for Slade's concept. First, the relationship of the teacher to the student was to be one of 'loving ally'. While that sounds reasonable, it causes practical concerns for the teacher. How does the loving ally strive for impartiality in assessment and evaluation? How does the teacher, charged with being non-intrusive, handle play that gets out of hand? What happens if students misbehave?

Slade's contribution was to acknowledge and prioritize the artistic ability of young children. His recognition of child drama as an art form in itself alerted teachers to the potential of the young child's drama making ability and its relationship with play. His work consolidated and strengthened the place of drama in the educational development of the child. The legacy of his work is seen in the existence of successful drama curriculum throughout the world for early childhood and primary students. Sladian technique may have been popular in the 1950s and 1960s, but it has been regarded with some scepticism since. In the current climate of literacy and numeracy testing regimes and outcomes-based learning, *Child Drama* seems remote; however, Slade's philosophies recognized strongly the ability of young children to create their own drama and influenced many that were to come after him.

Brian Way

Brian Way was an associate of Peter Slade. His book, *Development Through Drama* (1967), appears influenced by Slade's ideas about the potential for drama to develop the child. Way however remoulds drama inserting concepts that had hitherto not been included in drama education. Way states his personal development agenda upfront '. . . a basic definition of drama might be "simply to practise living"' (1967, p. 6). He states plainly early on in his book that: 'So far as it is humanly possible, this book is concerned with the development of people, not with the development of drama' (1967, p. 2).

He sees drama at the centre of the individual's development and as such he argues drama 'should be provided for every child and be the concern of every teacher' (1967, p. 6). This approach may sound similar to Dorothy Heathcote's 'living through drama' methods discussed later in this chapter. Way's *Development Through Drama* however contains several central differences. Way was primarily interested in the 'individuality of the individual' (1967, p. 3). Heathcote's approach was rather to teach her students about what it was to be a social being.

While Heathcote saw the theatre as being an important influence on her work as argued later, Way suggests that theatre has no real place in the development of his work: '. . . theatre is largely concerned with the *communication* between actors and an audience; drama is largely concerned with the experience by the participants, irrespective of any function of communication to an audience' (Way, 1967, p. 3).

Bolton conceptualizes Way's approach to teaching in terms of a 'physical education' style of teaching (Bolton, 1998, p. 149). Way used exercises that enabled the individual to practice the various skills important for development. His book has exercises that concentrate on, 'imagination', 'speaking', 'consciousness of self', 'self control' and so on. Way's approach to drama was to dissociate his concept from the theatre and prescribe a series of exercises that were designed to develop the individual. This approach appears to remove that which is educationally attractive about drama education and that was so much a part of the practice developed by Caldwell Cook. There was little place in Way's classroom for working with others to develop a 'we' feeling. There was a total disassociation from the audience. The creative play that Slade knew was replaced by ordered, assessed exercises, many of which had little or nothing to do with the theatre. In short, Way's personal development approach left drama with personal development and personal growth connotations. Slade's and Way's approaches seem far removed from the work of Dorothy Heathcote. Meanwhile, in the United States the creative dramatics movement was building its influence.

Winifred Ward

In the United States, one of the most influential figures in drama and education was the North-western University academic and teacher Winifred Ward. Her drama like Peter Slade's saw the role of drama as developing the whole child. Her aim was to give '. . . each child an avenue for self expression . . . and to give him opportunities to grow in self expression' (Ward, 1957, p. 4). Like the work of Slade and Way, the aesthetics of drama and theatre are displaced by the social learning opportunity that drama affords. Bolton ascribes the rise of the 'Creative Dramatics' movement to Ward's guidance and leadership of drama education in America. Her book *Creative Dramatics* (1930) outlines her philosophy and her belief that the arts added 'immeasurably to the joy of living' (1957, p. 5). Ward also opened a children's theatre that according to Helen Nicholson 'employed child actors with experience of improvisation and dramatic play on the basis that their acting technique had benefitted from this training' (2009, p. 16). One of the more recent leaders in the Creative Dramatics movement, Professor at New York University, Nellie McCaslin wrote just before her death in a retrospective piece:

> Is an aesthetic experience ever achieved in a creative drama class or in attending a performance of a children's play? Is theatre an art form worth studying in its own right or is it an educational tool, appealing to administrators and producers because it is effective? I believe that it is an art and should be taught as an art form first and foremost, but that skilfully done, it can accomplish both objectives. The grey area between art and education is difficult for the inexperienced teacher to negotiate without the loss of one goal or the other. It is the *intent* that charts the course. (McCaslin, 2005, p. 12)

The evolution of creative dramatics toward a more balanced view of process and product can be seen in McCaslin's reflections. Creative dramatics still has a voice in the American curriculum debate, but like drama in the United Kingdom and Australia it has evolved to take account of the aesthetic more centrally. Without doubt, however, the most dominant figure on the drama education landscape over the last 30 years is Dorothy Heathcote.

Dorothy Heathcote

Dorothy Heathcote's influence on drama education is profound and controversial. Many of the techniques she employed and promoted have now become drama education orthodoxy in schools (Mooney, 1989, p. 6). Her work also fostered several other theorists; most notably Cecily O'Neill, Betty Jane Wagner and Gavin Bolton to theorize around her work and develop frameworks that draw from her methodology. Even her harshest critic says of her and Gavin Bolton: 'It is impossible to embark on an examination of the complex texture of drama-in-education in the 1980s without acknowledging at an early stage the overarching presence of Dorothy Heathcote and Gavin Bolton' (Hornbrook, 1989, p. 16). Hornbrook rightly links Bolton and Heathcote, as Bolton's body of theoretical and practical work arises from the work of Heathcote. Hornbrook claims that Bolton gave Heathcote's 'highly intuitive methodology (a) respectable intellectual form' (1989, p. 19). While Hornbrook recognizes her contribution, he also sees much in her work to criticize. Primarily he argues that Heathcote created a mystical system that encouraged her followers to see her as a guru. However, what Hornbrook fails to recognize are the significant departures both O'Neill and Bolton have made from her work to develop approaches inspired by her practice (Bolton, 1998, p. 231).

Heathcote, like many of the others within drama education, was influenced by the theatre practice around her. She trained as an actor (Hodgson, 1972, p. 156) and would have been exposed to the work of Stanislavski[3] and Brecht[4] as part of her training. At one point she remarks about Brecht's work: 'I liked the notion of "that which will stand for this" –

because I play, you know I think that is deep play – that I can see what I'm making it out of. I love that' (Davis cited by Hornbrook, 1989, p. 17).

She quotes Brecht generously throughout her work to support her arguments, most particularly about 'we feeling' (1984, p. 13). Heathcote favoured the idea of practice in action: praxis. She explains, 'The Greek word for the practice of action is "praxis". We seem to have created in our syllabi very heavy stress upon thinking and very little stress on affective thinking. Drama is about affective thinking and cognitive thinking it is not just about behaviour' (Heathcote, 1984, p. 31).

Heathcote's 'living through drama'

In Heathcote's idea of 'living through drama', she encourages teachers and students to *do*. Heathcote sees drama as she claims the Greeks saw drama, 'to live through'. As early as 1972 (Hodgson, 1972, p. 157), she was articulating her work in terms of its social good, for instance living through, yet she was also justifying her work in terms of classical theatrical practice. She was attempting to embrace here the theatrical and the social. She says: 'A barrier has grown up and people have taken sides. The two teams are advocates of the so-called informal dramatics, whose creed is that children shall use their own language always, versus those who consider the so-called formal production is best . . . there is no reason why the two teams should necessarily be opposed' (Hodgson, 1972, p. 164).

This is a departure from much of the work of Slade and Way who sought early on to reject the theatre. Heathcote encourages the active; '. . . . First of all drama does – it does not teach about. We have to learn to make it do. Secondly it manufactures worlds which use all the known created knowledge . . .' Heathcote envisages drama as a way of creating worlds that help us understand our own, a dress rehearsal perhaps. Or as Hodgson (1972, p. 156) puts it, 'living through drama' is primarily about 'living through situations and the insight to be gained from them'. Bolton describes 'living through drama' developed from episode to episode by creating nested dramatic situations so that '. . . one "internal situation" breeding or "foreshadowing the next 'internal' situation", rather than "plot", whereas the latter prompts [plot] a "what-happens-next" mental set, the former is more conducive to "living through" operating at a seeming life rate, a modus vivendi that lent itself to staying with a situation sufficiently long to explore it and understand it more' (Bolton, 1998, p. 179).

Like Finlay-Johnson and Caldwell Cook, Heathcote promoted a radical change in teaching that had a 'doing' syllabus at its centre rather than a knowledge based syllabus. She maintains: 'I'm interested therefore, in making schools places where "doing" happens, particularly "public behaviour doing", the exploration of "celebration doing", "the consideration of what life is about doing", bonding and so on' (Heathcote, 1984, p. 33). Heathcote has more on her mind than the 'physical development model' espoused by Brian Way. She encourages the use of theatrical elements without a traditional audience to create worlds for students to learn. She is specific about what students will learn as well; not for Heathcote the vague feel good advocacy claim. She calls for drama educators to create evidence for their claims (Heathcote, 1984, p. 6).

This seems a long way from the 'mystifying language' Hornbrook[5] attributes to Heathcote's rise. On the contrary, Heathcote is very sure of what she is teaching and how she is teaching through drama. In Heathcote's *Man in a Mess* drama, a term which Bolton uses to describe her early work, she constructs a world and then invites students to take part in getting the 'mess' solved.

Heathcote and social interaction

Heathcote sees the world in terms of social interaction. She focuses on the 'we' rather than the 'I' or 'me' '. . . all the work of drama is about cultures and communities and about group systems. It is not a private art. It is a public art' (Heathcote, 1984, p. 25). The importance of this approach is that she defines drama unequivocally as an 'art' that depends on interaction. She creates worlds that are social, although virtual, that depend on the constructs of reality for their form. So when students examine a historical problem, it is not the dates and the facts that they examine in a Heathcote drama; it is the social relationships, the 'why' rather than the 'what'. It is also the construction of society that she is concerned with in the 'we feeling'. 'It is not me and it is not you, it is that which together this community makes in the spaces of communication we find between you and me and it is how society makes its social order' (Heathcote, 1984, p. 3). This understanding of the 'we' is drawn from the work of earlier educators, but the influence of Heathcote's theatrical training should not be discounted. She cites Brecht instructing actors: 'Your task, actors, is to be explorers and teachers of the art of dealing with people, knowing their nature and demonstrating it. You teach them to deal with themselves, you teach them the great art of living together' (Heathcote, 1984, p. 13).

The 'we' as central is a departure from the 'find a space on your own' school of drama teaching attributed by Bolton (1998, p. 151) to Brian Way. The focus on the communal, the ensemble is more in line with the work of Peter Slade and the earlier 'pioneers' Caldwell Cook and Finlay-Johnson. The other crucial difference from Brian Way's methodology was to move away from the 'physical education' style exercise to the entering of new worlds. Teachers trained on Way's *Development Through Drama* method must have been astounded at the innovation in Heathcote's approach. No longer was the approach 'exercises for living individually' but rather 'this is life, how do we fix it together?' As Bolton suggests,

> . . . Heathcote almost always worked with the whole class together in the initial stages of a new piece of work was more than an organisational preference. Her whole approach is based on a communal perspective, so that the pupils take on their roles primarily as 'we'. . . [1998, p. 186].

Heathcote is interested in how we make society and how we interact. Her work with such large groups (sometimes 30–40) is testament to her commitment. Her ability to maintain and create learning in 'the drama' attests to her skill as a powerful teacher-artist.

Heathcote's teacher in role

Teacher-in-role was another major contribution Heathcote made to modern practice. Bolton suggests that teacher-in-role, although probably influenced by her actor training and teaching experience, was distinctively Heathcotian. The teacher-in-role experience changed the power transaction between teacher and student by allowing the student to choose the role and status of the character. Teacher-in-role also depended on the student to provide the content of the drama rather than the teacher controlling the lesson.[6] The approach introduced a radical learning experience that took the teacher inside the drama.

As Bolton suggests, teachers were 'mystified' by teacher-in-role, some were more critical calling this approach 'indulgent and idiosyncratic' (Bolton, 1998, p. 182). Heathcote however worked with this technique to make the dramatic worlds she was creating authentic. It is one thing for students to create belief in a situation, but quite another to collaborate with your teacher and create the same belief or authenticity. The teacher-in-role technique was a logical extension of the new teacher to student relationship she urged; 'In drama the teacher in a way suffers a reversal of his usual role, which is that of one who knows . . . Therefore he [the student] is not asking the teacher for the answer, he is offering the teacher a viewpoint and in return the teacher may offer another one. Neither one will be right or wrong' (Hodgson, 1972, p. 160).

This approach saw the power relationship alter. There was an equal understanding and even though the teacher led the group, the student's experiences were valued. In her New Zealand lectures in 1984, Heathcote decried the loss of power of the child. She argued that child labour reforms had an unintended outcome: 'the disenfranchisement of the power of children to be a productive, positive influence in our society' (Heathcote 1984, p. 6). Heathcote is calling here for a realignment of the relationship between teacher and student. Teacher-in-role was a major part of that approach.

> The roles that Heathcote takes are those that give her the greatest maneuverability. Her favourite ones are middle-rank positions: the first mate, the foreman in the factory, the police officer who is just following orders, the radio transmitter on a submarine, Caesar's messenger, the doctor's assistant. This way she is not the final power, but she is the effect of the power . . . she wants ample power, but not the power to make final decisions. (Wagner, 1979, p. 129)

This description comes from Betty Jane Wagner who observed Heathcote's practice and wrote sometimes-florid descriptions of her work. Hornbrook (1984, p. 18) uses these descriptions to make much of his case about the mysticism of Heathcote's practice, criticisms that may have been more accurately attributed to the observer (Wagner) rather than to the observed (Heathcote).

Heathcote's work related something very new in drama education, the teacher controlling the drama by becoming part of the action.[7] In this mode the teacher created and facilitated a virtual world by becoming part of it. Students were invested with real power to make decisions about the drama. No longer did a spot on the floor or words on the page dictate the drama. The power relationship was reconfigured. Paradoxically, and perhaps against Heathcote's wishes, many saw the power relationship shifting further to the teacher, who with the added impetus of role could step outside the bounds of teacher behaviour. However *Three Looms Waiting* (BBC, 1976) does show a teacher (Heathcote) demonstrating a very teacher-led classroom. Certainly teacher-in-role introduced a new power relationship, but whether it reduced the power of the teacher in favour of empowering students is still an open question. As Bolton says that teacher in role '. . . clearly invests the teacher with considerable power. When she starts her role, she is, as it were, "holding all the cards". . . if seen as unexpected behaviour of a teacher, it increases the teacher's power potential' (Bolton, 1998, p. 183).

Bolton goes on to observe that Heathcote's later work attempted to change this power relationship. As Bolton observes, 'the role of the teacher is that of dramatist, a dramatist who is not only supplying the words but the accompanying non-verbal signals, so that the reading required of the pupils is multi-dimensional' (Bolton, 1998, p. 184). In this description, we see the unifying force of Heathcote's praxis. She encourages the teacher to engage with the art form personally to help her students engage with it. In this one technique, she embraces theatre and teaching. However, there are several issues that arise from Heathcote's teacher-in-role method. Initially as Bolton suggests (1998, p. 185), the drama is teacher-led. It does not really become successful until the students make their own 'interpretations'. There is a danger also that teachers could subsume the power and deliver no real benefit except their own ego gratification.

Mantle of the expert

These concerns about student power led Heathcote to develop the concept of 'Mantle of the Expert'. This technique allows the teacher to work on the drama from the inside and delivers power to the students. As Bolton (1989, p. 240) says: 'To understand Heathcote's approach, one needs to understand that where the participants themselves are required to take on the role in improvised as opposed to scripted work, she sees no alternative to helping them "from the inside" by taking on a role herself'. 'Mantle of the Expert' creates roles for students that cast them as the 'ones who know' (instead of the teacher). For example, a student may take on the role of a scientist whose expertise is required to solve a problem in outer space. The expertise role shifts the power from the teacher to the student.

In 'Mantle of the Expert', Heathcote designed a teaching technique that invites the teacher to support the learning by making the teacher the insider, supporting the work of the students as the experts. This radical change in the classroom power setup is designed to give students the status and the responsibility of expertise. Heathcote explains in Bolton (1998, p. 240) why she uses this strategy: 'I began to realize that the expertise of viewpoint could help teachers with little conscious understanding of theatre to get things started *under* the story line instead of merely replicating narrative'.

Heathcote is interested in the ways 'play' can be adapted within the bounds of teacher-in-role. Her commitment to play like that of her predecessors is fundamental. 'The ability to play seriously is fundamental. It is the mark of the artist and scientist, the inventor and all innovators' (Heathcote, 1984, p. 25). Her approach to teacher-in-role and mantle of the expert was always based on the attempt to create authentic experiences in virtual worlds.

Unsurprisingly, Heathcote had both extremely strong admirers and strong critics. David Hornbrook's criticisms appear to be more related to the manner rather than the method. Here he is speaking about the commentary on Heathcote's work by Bolton and Wagner:

> The trouble with this mode of discourse is that it obscures the vital distinction we must always make between the utterance and the utterer if we are to attempt a constructive evaluation of what is being said. The employment of first names, avuncular familiarity, the selective use of critical judgement, make it almost impossible to prise the text from the personality. In a blur of disciplinary defensiveness, Gavin becomes inseparable from Gavin's theories; to challenge the idea is to threaten the person. (Hornbrook, 1989, p. 20)

There is some truth in Hornbrook's claim. Obviously Heathcote's work drew followers, as it was new and for some, breathtaking. One needs only to read some of the commentary by Betty Jane Wagner to observe the rapturous, almost uncritical approach some observers employed. Furthermore, the use of first names contributed to the impression by some in theoretical circles that the work lacked rigour. However, these criticisms do not go to the heart of the work; they are however, reprimanding Heathcote's lack of respect (Hornbrook says 'ability'), for the academic and theoretical world.

His second charge is that drama education that constituted a radical change to classroom practice could not be evaluated or assessed. He argued that to assess work in drama is to measure how compliant students are (1989, p. 26). His criticism is that Heathcote's work demands compliance in students. He takes his example from Lance and Martyn (Hornbrook, 1989, p. 26) who set up a framework for assessment that has some serious problems, not the least of which is their attempt to measure compliance. Others such as Cecily O'Neill (1995), Jonathan Neelands (1990) and John Thompson (1991) in Australia have devised far more satisfactory approaches that Hornbrook has neglected to include in his arguments. Heathcote's approach to drama required a kind of social cohesion. To succeed, students needed to work with others and the teacher-in-role. What Hornbrook misses in his criticisms is the nature of assessment when working with interpersonal relationships. Surely Hornbrook would agree that an actor who works in an ensemble needs to be able to work with his/her fellow actors. This skill is also required by the students in Heathcote's classes and as such should be assessed.

How does one sum up the impact of Dorothy Heathcote's work and what influence does she have on modern drama practice? One of her strongest advocates, Gavin Bolton says, 'Dorothy Heathcote has found a way of bringing the power of make-believe into the classroom so that her pupils can be "inside the skin of the expert" and enjoy his sense of joyous intellectual adventure using . . . an enterprise culture' (1998, p. 244).

In terms of criticism, perhaps her harshest published critic, David Hornbrook says that Heathcote and Bolton '. . . succeeded in providing far more than a new methodology for the teaching of drama . . . they offered a wisdom that claimed its origins in deep spiritual truth and a unifying vision of humanity which absolved their followers from further moral or ideological speculation' (1984, p. 28). There is some truth in both of these summaries of her work. She brought the worlds of education and theatre together to create a genuinely new pedagogy and her approaches still have a profound impact on teachers (O'Toole et al., 2009). Teachers use her methods to create authentic experiences for their students to learn about the real world in which they live and create new ones to provide distance and other perspectives on their current reality. Some teachers use Heathcotian techniques without even being aware of their source.

Gavin Bolton

Gavin Bolton is closely associated with Heathcote. In *2D,* the editor offers the following tribute;

> Heathcote once described herself 'burrowing along like a mole in the dark' meaning I think that she pursued her own obsessions as a teacher. She contrasted her own inwardness with Gavin Bolton's capacity to see 'a large landscape and the patterns of it'. Well, moles may not **see** the landscape, but they change it, and the change Heathcote has wrought upon the drama landscape is no less than a transformation . . . (Anon, 1986, p. 81)

This 'farewell' neatly articulates the standing, relationship and the character of Heathcote and Bolton's partnership. It communicates the awe with which she was regarded and gives some weight to the 'guru' tag that Hornbrook (1989, p. 19) argues her followers gave her. It also recognizes Heathcote's singular talents and her 'obsessions'. Most importantly, however, it describes the link between Heathcote and Bolton. While Heathcote reshapes the terrain, Bolton soars over it. Thus the relationship is defined, the practitioner and the theoretician.[8]

Gavin Bolton's role in shaping the terrain and not just observing it is however far more important than this metaphor might suggest. Bolton's theories and practice extended Heathcote's work and enabled others to apply her teaching in their own classrooms. His codifying and theorizing of Heathcote began a tradition that continues in Betty Jane Wagner, John Carroll, Cecily O'Neill, Jonothan Neelands, John O'Toole and Brad Haseman's writing, to provide ways into Heathcote practice and to make it useable and accessible.

Bolton's view is that process drama is the dominant and most important form of classroom drama: 'The content of a drama lesson is interdisciplinary . . . [students of all ages] may have their understandings of the world clarified or modified and secondly they may gain skills in social interaction which include the ability to communicate their understandings and feelings' (Bolton, 1980, p. 71). Here Bolton outlines an approach to drama education that absolutely raises process over product. He later in this chapter describes the perfect drama class and states four expectations of the class, the fourth expectation being: 'They know it is an art form "*in process* not product"' (Bolton, 1980, p. 74). Bolton opposes, at this stage in his career, the role of acting in classroom drama that leads to product. His approach is to support the Heathcotian notion of 'living through' drama and sees the drama as the problem to be solved (Bolton, 1980, p. 72).

Bolton and trust

One of Bolton's major contributions is his ability to articulate ways for teachers to understand and use Heathcotian techniques with their classes. Bolton articulates some principles for teaching drama in the classroom being trust, protection, negotiation of meaning and containing emotion (Bolton, 1980, pp. 78–86). He argues that the first task of the drama teacher is to establish trust. He describes the competing agendas of a demonstration class he led where he needed to negotiate the lesson away from the student's games and performance agendas and toward Bolton's interest in process; 'From the very start the children at Riverside found themselves in a situation they could not trust, not simply because of the place and the milling throng of adults, but because of the expectations of drama that they brought with them' (1980, p. 79).

Having detected a trust problem, Bolton addressed the issue by allowing the students to choose the theme of the drama and work within the topic he chose. He progresses the process by developing a protection for students. He says 'So the only way it seems to me is to "protect" them into a context that does not expose, a context that naturally permits them to indulge an "introverting" emotion while gradually opening up the topic'. (1980, p. 81)

Bolton uses protection into role to insulate his students from inauthentic 'acting'. He argues that protection allows students eventually to work with a 'feeling quality' creatively. Later he speaks of protection, not as a way to stop emotion but rather a way to launch into emotions that are useful to the drama; 'By protection then we do not mean protection from emotion, but rather a carefully structured projection into emotion so that participants are engaged but not threatened' (Bolton, 1986, p. 22). Recently, leading Norwegian drama educator Stig Eriksson in his book *Distancing at Close Range* (2009) wrote comprehensively about trust, distancing and the links between key theatrical movements and modern drama practice tracing this lineage through the work of Bolton and Heathcote. This work contextualizes the work of Bolton and points to its roots in theatrical aesthetic and perhaps more importantly the potential distancing has to expand and enrich classroom drama and deepen the dramatic meaning inherent in learning.

Negotiating meaning

Negotiation of meaning is the phase in process drama where the 'delicate uncovering process occurs' (Bolton, 1980, p. 81). Here there is a negotiation between teacher and student about what the meaning will be. Bolton describes his work with students exploring 'violence in schools'. He negotiates meaning in this instance by not overlaying student perceptions of the topic with his own. The next phase in negotiating meaning in Bolton's example was to clarify the meaning. He says of the students, 'so what they are not really after *violence* as such but some form of *school illegality*' (1980, p. 82). This negotiation like any teacher to student negotiation has power relationships within it. This raises questions about how negotiated the meaning actually is in this approach, or if it is teacher transmitted. Bolton's agendas seem pedagogically sound to reshape the work of the students to create more satisfactory learning outcomes. There is however some doubt over whether these changes were negotiated or imposed.

Bolton's final stage is containing and harnessing the emotion. Bolton uses this phase as a safeguard against students becoming emotionally vulnerable in the drama and as a way of creating an emotional authenticity. He began by removing the situation from the students' real class and school to a fictitious class and school. Bolton says 'I insisted that we were in some other school – and with a class with an unfamiliar title. Another safeguard lies in the tightness of teacher structuring' (1980, p. 84).

Here Bolton is summing up what seem to be his theories and contribution to drama education's theory and practice. He is providing structure for teachers to use and defines emotion at the centre of his work. He has provided new approaches to exploring Heathcote's work. Rather than imitating her, he creates structures to progress the work. In summing up his work with Riverside, he then speaks about what students learn through his work and he defines it with his structures '. . . trust; protection; negotiation of meaning and containing'. He says: 'It seems to me that the art of acting is the drawing out of an emotional response in an audience. For the child in the drama, the skill lies in behaving with integrity and spontaneity in a fictitious situation, not acting in the sense just described, but *being . . .*' (1980, p. 86).

The difficulty with Bolton's characterization of the difference between 'acting' and 'being' here is that he is discussing poor acting. In reality there is, as he agrees in his later writing (Bolton, 1998), acting in process drama and authenticity in the best type of acting. The opposition of: 'acting' and 'being' created a false dichotomy between the process and the product of classroom drama.

In his introduction to *Acting in Classroom Drama* he says:

> It is my intention to both provide an historical perspective and to propose a reformulation of classroom acting behaviour . . . .
>
> This reformulation attempts to make a case for embracing, in the classroom, many different kinds of acting behaviours that go beyond the limits and responsibilities of a stage actor, with nevertheless including both 'stage' acting and that kind of acting behaviour associated with 'teacher-in-role' led drama . . . (Bolton 1998, p. XVII)

Bolton's change of view recognizes that theatre and drama education were not natural enemies and that one might support the other.

Bolton also participated in some of the major debates that still occupy the discussions and arguments of drama educators. The process versus product argument, ignited through Slade's *Child Drama*, is renewed through Bolton's exploration of the relationship between drama and theatre. The most interesting characteristic of his work in this area is his ability to shift his view to lead and embrace the changing trends in drama and education.

Since Bolton has documented and analysed Heathcote's work, he has been identified as the theoretician while Heathcote has been cast in the role of the practitioner. This is not however a fair reflection of the work of Bolton. His work and theories stand for themselves and his theoretical shifts reflect many of the intellectual tensions in drama education. Bolton's work provides structure and links Heathcote's work back to the theatre, but not, in Bolton's thinking, to acting. He also teaches his students about 'dramatic process', 'dramatic form' and 'integrity of feeling'. His approaches begin the development of frameworks that endure and introduce a substantial attempt to theorize and make accessible the work of Heathcote. The other major contribution is his insistence on process, while simultaneously allowing a discussion of theatrical form. His recognition of the importance of form opens the way for the blending of theatre arts and process drama. This is extraordinary in that at this time he was still rejecting the place of acting in process drama. He concludes his chapter by arguing that[9]: 'The structures that are available to a teacher in carrying out both functions are often the structures employed by the playwright. A drama teacher is consistently working in Theatre form' (1980, p. 87).

After Heathcote

The analysis and description of form and structure was a preoccupation of several drama educators who wrote to respond and clarify the work of Heathcote and Bolton. These educators sought to provide structure to the concepts and practice that Heathcote and Bolton introduced and theorized to aid teachers planning drama learning. There are many drama educators who could fall under this category, but I have concentrated on those who have had the greatest influence on my work and practice. In these theorists, researchers and practitioners (many fulfilled all three roles), we also see the internationalization of drama education. The discussion of these figures begins with an examination of the contribution of Gavin Bolton's student Cecily O'Neill.

Cecily O'Neill

O'Neill was, as many others were, deeply influenced by the work of Heathcote and Bolton. Writing in 1995, she calls their '. . . understanding of the power of drama as a medium for learning as well as an art form was enormously influential . . . . Almost all I know about drama I learned from these two outstanding theorists and practitioners . . .' (Taylor, 1995, p. 4). O'Neill's contribution was to elucidate and extend the work of Heathcote and Bolton; it was an '. . . attempt to clarify some of what we had learned from Bolton and Heathcote and make it accessible for teachers' (Taylor, 1995, p. 4).

She also attempts in her structures to re-situate Drama in Education, or as she later calls it process drama[10] within a theatrical context. She says 'Drama in education has the capacity to expose the key dramatic structures and characteristics it shares with other kinds of theatre . . . the ephemeral and unpredictable process which is intrinsically dramatic, truly educational and profoundly worthwhile' (Taylor, 1995, p. 4).

O'Neill's conceptualization of drama in education is that of a structured learning enterprise that helps students explore the world around them. Writing in 1982 with Alan Lambert, she defines her view of drama: 'Drama in education is a mode of learning. Through the pupils' active identification with imagined roles and situations in drama, they can learn to explore issues, events and relationships. In drama, children draw on their knowledge and experience of the real world in order to create a make-believe world' (Lambert and O'Neill, 1982, p. 11).

In *Drama Structures,* O'Neill and Lambert (1982) provide structures around the work of Bolton and Heathcote by detailing fifteen defined frameworks for the development of drama lessons and programs. Despite the title of the book, the structures she creates reflect the development of drama worlds rather than simply providing technical scaffolding to assist with the mechanics of the drama. Her dramas use exercises and stimulus materials to transport teachers and students to worlds outside their own reality such as 'The Lost Valley', 'Starship' and 'Emigrants' (Lambert and O'Neill, 1982, p. 5). The intent of these structures was to provide teachers with explicit approaches for developing drama in their own classroom. The very existence of this book in 1982 suggests that those structures were not immediately obvious to teachers in the work of Heathcote and Bolton themselves. In the foreword to *Drama Structures,* Bolton praises the book for its ability to be applied easily: 'But the greatest achievement of this book is that it sets out to *teach*. The reader is not only able to follow what happened in someone else's teaching, he or she is presented at critical points with a close analysis of the choices open to the teacher concerned' (Lambert and O'Neill, 1982, p. 7).

O'Neill's achievement here according to Bolton is the presentation of a resource that not only depicts the teaching methodology like the influential Heathcote BBC videos (BBC, 1976), but shows teachers how to analyse and structure their own drama teaching. The book also marked a recognition that drama educators needed to conform to cross-curricular standards and explain their methodology. As Bolton comments:

> the authors recognise that for teaching drama in this decade teachers need to adopt a more trenchant rationale and methodology: they must acquire a much wider range of techniques including teacher-in-role and (so important) teacher not in role; a stronger sense of what is essential to theatre form; a more sophisticated notion of drama for learning and, above all, a new respect for the 'content' or 'themes' for which drama can be the vehicle. (O'Neill and Lambert, 1982, p. 7)

These structures provided drama teachers with models that they could replicate that were consistent with the work of Heathcote and Bolton. The book, as Bolton says, sets out to teach and as such deconstruct the complexity of drama teaching methodology. These structures provided accessible and teachable lessons and programs. These programs went some way in refuting the claims that drama in education was predicated on 'mysticism and midwifery' and not accessible to ordinary teachers (Hornbrook, 1989, p. 18). In O'Neill's structures, Heathcote's approaches are analysed and demonstrated in a simple and straightforward manner for teachers of all abilities and levels of experience to teach. On the other hand, O'Neill's structures were perhaps too easy to replicate. Teachers could now use her structures, coming as they did with their own cultural and personal orientations, as drama. This may not have been O'Neill's intent, but the scarcity of other tangible and accessible material allowed some teachers to displace their own curriculum development to reproduce established lessons developed by O'Neill (Haseman, 2001, p. 1). *Drama Structures* was however an important contribution to making drama more structured and available for ordinary teachers despite the drawbacks associated with its sometimes unsatisfactory implementation.

By 1995, O'Neill's approach to drama education had evolved further. She says of *Drama Structures* that the satisfying dramatic events that arise from these structures do not necessarily occur because of their relationship to:

> specific or educational purposes. They are most effective when they obey the intrinsic rules of the dramatic event. *Drama Structures* is one of several publications that have helped teachers to moderate the unpredictability of improvisation by structuring and developing the dramatic encounter through a sequence of episodes. My purpose in this book is rather different. I hope to clarify the relationship between what I call process drama and the basic characteristics of the theatre event. (O'Neill, 1995, p. xiv)

The other important development in *Drama Worlds* is her description and use of the term process drama.

> Process drama is a complex dramatic encounter. Like other theatre events, it evokes an immediate dramatic world bounded in space and time, a world that depends on the consensus of all those present for its existence . . . . Process drama shares the key features of every theatre event and is articulated through the same kinds of dramatic organization. (O'Neill, 1995, p. xii)

In this definition O'Neill includes the traditions of drama in education and its attendant process and the importance of working with the central elements of the theatre, audience, staging, dramatic tension and so on. O'Neill's acceptance and promotion of this term avoids the false dichotomy of the process versus product argument explored earlier. In her view, both are important. Rather than rejecting theatrical form, she embraces it as part of the process drama. She says: 'Process drama is structured and developed in the same way that dramatic worlds occur in the theatre, and participation in the creation of these worlds can be intrinsically satisfying, educationally worthwhile and dramatically significant' (O'Neill, 1995, p. xx).

O'Neill here is articulating a form that has both aesthetic value and educational value. Process drama, in her view, allows students to create their own worlds and present them in a way that has artistic and social value. True to her original intent in *Drama Structures* (O'Neill and Lambert, 1985), O'Neill is providing structures that assist teachers to make drama more accessible for their students. In 1993, she coined the term 'pre-text' to describe a particular type of stimulus used to begin drama. She describes the concept as: '. . . clarifying the means by which the drama world is set in motion. Pre-text refers to the source or impulse for the drama process . . . . As well as indicating an excuse, – a reason for the work – it also carries the meaning of the text that exists before the event' (O'Neill, 1995, p. xv). Again, she is striving for structure within her dramatic activities. The pre-text provides order for an improvisation and establishes the field within which the drama will take place. Pam Scheurer observed O'Neill's practice and commented on her structuring process. 'My observations of O'Neill reveal that she does engage in a complex and dynamic style of planning that requires both intellectual and creative processes' (1998, p. 32). O'Neill is consistently making structural decisions during her teaching of drama and her practice and publications have provided teachers also with the tools to structure their teaching in this subject. The addition of pretext has given teachers another strategy for structuring improvisation and the drama education process. Her theory and practice have made drama more accessible and manageable for teachers and consequently, her strategies and structures have become commonplace in syllabus and curriculum development. Like Cecily O'Neill, Jonothan Neelands has also contributed important structures for drama educators to use in their classrooms.

Jonothan Neelands

Jonothan Neelands is another drama educator influenced by Heathcote's practice. In 1984, he described his view of drama in Heathcotian terms as not being about the theatre but rather reflecting through social interactions and human meaning (Neelands, 1984, p. 6). His book *Structuring Drama Work* (1990) provided teachers with strategies they could use with their students to teach conventions of the theatre. This use of the term 'theatre' is consistent with O'Neill's use of the term process drama to include the '. . . developments in contemporary theatre' (O'Neill, 1995, p. xvii). Neelands identifies four types of dramatic action:

1. context building action,
2. narrative action,
3. poetic action, and
4. reflective action.

He is attempting to define the processes of dramatic action and develop strategies for teachers that will assist them to teach the progression of dramatic action as well as its components. He says this work provides: '. . . the conventions that make up the "palate" that teachers/leaders and students use in theatre; the application of the palate to create a picture requires those skills of sensitivity, perception and craft which develop through practical involvement and experimentation in theatre itself' (Neelands, 1990, p. 4).

Like O'Neill, Neelands emerges from a Heathcotian[11] pedagogical position, but rejects the false dichotomies of process versus product and theatre versus drama. This more eclectic approach, in his view, 'opens up' the field of drama education. He broadened this even further to include non-English traditions at the second International conference of IDEA[12] in Brisbane in 1995: '. . . a new trans-cultural paradigm of theatre is needed that will encompass the process drama tradition within a broader field of theatre which acknowledges both the Euro-American performance tradition and other "rich traditions" as well . . .' (Neelands, 1996, p. 24).

Neelands here identifies the merit in exploring the wealth of all traditions and placing the process drama within a broader, more intercultural field. His attraction to the use of the theatre is central and clear. In 1997, he said: 'Theatre is understood through its conventions which are the indications of the ways in which time, space and presence can interact and be imaginatively shaped to create different kinds of meanings' (1998, p. 10).

Recently *Creating Democratic Citizenship* (O'Connor, 2010) tracked the life and work of Jonothan Neelands through reflections on his practice and writing by himself and other prominent drama practitioners. Neelands' particular gift has been to hold the pedagogical and the political together as he discusses drama education as a site for democratic change and knowledge. Juliana Saxton reflecting on his work in this book says 'Neelands' theatre provides both place *and* space where, after doing and re-doing reflecting and reflecting and re-doing until we are filled up, we can begin to see ourselves as actors and agents; where questions wait for us to find them where in "acting to learn", we learn to act' (O'Connor, 2010, p. 169). Another drama educator who strove to connect drama education to the world of ideas was Richard Courtney.

Richard Courtney

The move toward a more theoretically connected understanding in the field can be credited to a large degree to the work of Richard Courtney. His substantial body of work positioned drama education within the fields of sociology and philosophy, so much so that John O'Toole argues that he was '. . . effectively drama education's first philosopher' (O'Toole et al., 2009, p. 197). He connected the ritualistic and symbolic features of drama education in an effort to reconcile the pedagogic with the aesthetic (that had been disconnected in the process versus product schisms). In his book, *Drama and Feeling: An Aesthetic Theory* (1995), he produced a philosophical position for drama education. He says: 'The symbolic power of dramatic action lies in its ability to effectively construct worldviews. It creates ideas of "the way things are". At least partially it legitimizes the cultural order. But it can simultaneously provide symbolic models to change this order' (1998, p. 138). Courtney's legacy of rich and abundant scholarship demands more space than I have here. There is however in his writing much that will feed the field and generate discussion as drama education continues evolving. Norah Morgan and Julianna Saxton continue the move towards inclusive curriculum in drama.

Norah Morgan and Juliana Saxton

In common with many other drama educators of their day, Norah Morgan and Juliana Saxton adhere to the concepts outlined by Heathcote and Bolton (Morgan and Saxton, 1987, p. 2). They take an eclectic approach to drama and theatre as well as process and product (1987, p. 1) while providing strategies for making drama education structures clear and accessible. Their book, *Teaching Drama: A Mind of Many Wonders* (1987) concentrates on clarifying Heathcotian structures such as teacher-in-role and mantle of the expert among others and making the techniques more transparent (1987, p. 38 and p. 107). One of their main contributions, however, has been in the development of an understanding of the centrality of questioning techniques in drama. They identify the drama question as:

- showing genuine curiosity;
- occurring in a context that relates to the drama experience;
- supporting the students and/or the teacher-in-role;
- being supported by the intonation and non-verbal signals of the questioner;
- making the pace of the question relate to the situation.

Their contribution here has been to deconstruct and explain the methodology of questioning in Heathcotian drama, practiced by Heathcote and others like Cecily O'Neill (Morgan and Saxton, 1987, p. 81) and to make its processes and techniques transparent and useful for the teacher. Furthermore, Morgan and Saxton are exploring the role of questioning within general teaching pedagogy.[13] More importantly, however, like the other drama educators mentioned here, they are defining the unique features of drama questions and in detail how questions can be applied to structure, devise, shape and extend the drama. Most recently Saxton has continued her prolific output through presentation throughout the world with her collaborator and leading drama educator, Carole Miller. She has also extended this work further publishing in applied drama and theatre fields as to her complementery work in drama education.

John O'Toole

John O'Toole's contribution has been to define the space for drama education and introduce the elements of dramatic form into the teaching of drama. His approach to drama resembles Heathcote in that in his words: '. . . as drama people, we are concerned about human behaviour, social issues and ethical questions – they're the stuff of drama' (O'Toole, 1998, p. 15).

He also provides structures and tools to help drama teachers to develop their own work and rejects as others do the 'false dichotomies' of process versus product, instead preferring the term, process drama. O'Toole sums up his position: '. . . to control the elements of drama and manage active participants who are usually quite inexperienced in drama – in order to create a powerful and pleasurable learning experience, especially in a classroom full of desks or a marketplace full of street vendors[14] – is an aesthetic challenge that demands dramatic skills of the highest order . . .' (O'Toole, 1998, p. 15).

In his book, *The Process of Drama: Negotiating Art and Meaning* (1992) he articulates the elements of drama and defines what he calls the 'territory' (O'Toole, 1992, p. 2) of drama.

> One of the main ideas in the book is that drama is not literature, words on a page. That is just a play-script, and the same relationship to drama as a score has to music. Drama itself *happens* and never accidentally; it is a dynamic event which is always part of its context. Since schools form an important part of the context in which this genre usually happens, schooling practices and educational ideas and structures do feature prominently, as a background to the aesthetic. (O'Toole, 1992, p. 1)

The clarification, explanation and potential uses of the elements of drama explained by O'Toole articulated much that had been innate in good drama teaching and provided a vocabulary, so teachers could teach and explain the mechanisms at work in the drama. This tool, like the structures of O'Neill and Neelands, invited teachers to explore the workings of the drama and manipulate the dramatic action. He identifies the elements of drama and says: 'They are not just the basis of our body of knowledge. Through them we give the students the tools of the trade. And it is to do with empowerment' (O'Toole, 1998, p. 15).

O'Toole's identification of the elements was made available to teachers through his work with Brad Haseman on what is now a drama classroom classic, *Dramawise: An Introduction to the Elements of Drama* (Haseman and O'Toole, 1986). *Dramawise* explained and outlined the elements of drama[15] and described how they could be taught in the classroom. O'Toole explains how the elements of drama can demystify the dramatic process:

> We identified some elements [of drama] and showed them all working, both in conventional theatre and in process drama. We thought it important to teach young people these elements – this is the basis of our body of knowledge . . . Our effort was simplistic but I still find our list of the elements useful myself, artistically and as a teacher. I use it as a checklist when I am teaching or rehearsing and if it's not going well: what have I overlooked – the dramatic tension? the use of space? careful enough characterization? is it the timing and the tempo? I can usually identify where I am going wrong. (O'Toole, 1998, p. 15)

John O'Toole's contribution bridged the process and product divide by recognizing and valuing both approaches. His ability to define, analyse and provide teaching strategies (especially the elements of drama), provided valuable pedagogical insights. The legacy of this work can be seen in syllabus documents and in drama classrooms internationally. His work avoids false divisions and delivers to teachers and students tools to understand and manipulate form as well as undertake social learning through the drama. Another who led by looking beyond the field was Australia's John Carroll.

John Carroll

In a book that deals with teaching drama in the twenty-first century, it would be an oversight to omit John Carroll. John Carroll's particular ability has been to see the advances in other fields and bring these perspectives to enrich and deepen the scholarship of drama education. He has the distinction of being Dorothy Heathcote's only PhD student. His background as a linguist provided him with the disciplinary background to systematically and theoretically ground his understanding of classroom drama practice. His research since the mid-1980s in emergent digital performance forms, online videogames and drama culminating in *Real Players* in 2006 (Carroll, Anderson and Cameron, 2006) has led the field. His research and scholarship in role protection and role distance provided teachers with an understanding of the importance of these processes in the classroom. Most recently he has built on this work to engage drama education with digital game development (Anderson, Cameron and Carroll, 2009). John Carroll's contribution has been to see the shifts in drama education mostly before anyone else and creating a place for drama education researchers to pursue new possibilities across disciplinary boundaries.

These drama educators have contributed clarity and accessibility to the work of the drama in education pioneers, especially Heathcote and Bolton. Their various structures, techniques, strategies and tools have allowed teachers to deconstruct Heathcote and Bolton's work and develop their own practice. They have contributed to the ongoing health and development of this subject area. They have provided drama teachers with structures and techniques that simplify and explicate Heathcote's approach and demonstrate its application in the classroom.

The legacy of the pioneers – Heathcote and Bolton and the post-Heathcotians mentioned here – have had a significant impact on the development of curriculum internationally. These drama educators have contributed to a subject area that now has a theoretical base that is accessible and useful for teaching. This journey has seen the pioneers introducing concepts that made the way clear for the innovation and excitement of drama in education introduced by Dorothy Heathcote and Gavin Bolton. Their work, which was a major turning point, was later deconstructed and made accessible by those who sturctured and added to Heathcote's work. Their influence has also seen the diminution of the debates over process and product and drama versus theatre as these practitioners recognize the dangers of false dichotomies and the value of an eclectic approach to drama education. Before we leave the history of drama education, we must discuss the 'new kid on the block': applied theatre.

The rise and rise of applied theatre

Applied theatre is frequently defined as theatre work conducted outside of conventional mainstream theatre houses for the purpose of transforming or changing human behaviour.

Applied theatre is characterized by its desire to influence human activity, to raise issues and have audience members problem-solve those issues (Taylor, 2003). Perhaps Ackroyd (1999) comes closest to an encompassing definition:

> [Applied theatre] . . . practitioners share a belief in the power of the theatre form to address something beyond the form itself. So one group uses theatre in order to promote positive social processes within a particular community, while others employ it in order to promote an understanding of human resource issues among corporate employees. The range is huge, including such as theatre for education, for community development and for health promotion, and dramatherapy and psychodrama. (Ackroyd, 1999)

Nicholson (2006) most succinctly defines the field as '. . . dramatic activity that primarily exists outside conventional mainstream theatre institutions, which [is] specifically intended to benefit individuals, communities and societies'.

Applied theatre in action

Applied Theatre has grown from the roots of drama education and community theatre. The practice and approaches of Augusto Boal and Dorothy Heathcote are equally evident in the practice of contemporary applied theatre practitioners. The aspiration of Jonothan Neelands and Dorothy Heathcote mentioned earlier in this chapter for the development of a transformative and dynamic pedagogy has escaped schools and permeated community work, hospitals, businesses, jails and other non-school settings. In nurse education, the Drama Caring and Reflecting (DRACAR) project in Sweden (Ekebergh, 2004) aimed to bridge the perceived gap between theory and practice in nurse education (Lepp, 2000). Applied theatre practitioners engaged participants in ways that developed deep understanding about the key issues relating to nursing practice. Nursing students participated in strategies including role-play, forum theatre[16] and improvisation to explore and reflect on real life experiences from situations arising in clinical practice. The outcomes of this process indicate that drama and reflective activity facilitated learning through supervised dramatic fictional settings that '. . . enabled students to integrate experiences of care with caring theory' (Dahlberg, Ekebergh and Lepp, 2004, p. 627). 'Bodily' engagement with their learning allowed these students to develop a profound understanding of the patient's *life-view*. The students '. . . described how drama and the reflective activity gave them different forms of expression and enabled them to gain a greater understanding of the enigma of care . . . that [it] enabled them to encounter the patients and their lifeworld' (Dahlberg, Ekebergh and Lepp, 2004, p. 627). The cooling conflict program (O'Toole et al., 2005) used these techniques to combat bullying in Australian schools and the Drama for Conflict Management (DRACON) has been achieving similar aims in Norway and Sweden. Peter O'Connor's work using improvisation, role-play and music to support the rehabilitation of young offenders in jails sits alongside his work in schools using the same techniques to combat family violence. The strategies are the same because they have been trialled and developed in large part through drama education's history. What applied theatre has allowed is the application of these robust and engaging strategies to contexts that may not be schools. For teachers, the opportunity for community engagement is very exciting. The skills that are used to teach drama in schools effectively are readily transferable to other settings. Applied theatre has allowed practitioners to research and apply these strategies to create the potential for transformative learning and critical hope (Friere, 2004) in schools and beyond. While there is much opportunity in the rise of Applied Theatre, some tensions have also arisen with drama education.

Tensions between applied theatre and drama education

The relationship between drama and applied theatre has not always been harmonious. While there have been many in the field who work in drama education and applied theatre, there has also been a tendency on the behalf of some on both sides to attempt to disengage drama education from applied theatre. For example, Dalrymple discussing the Dramaide program argues '. . . "Applied Theatre" refers to the practice of drama and theatre-based activities outside the formal school curriculum' (Dalrymple, 2006, p. 201). Dalrymple argues in her footnotes that the exclusion is because the outcomes of the curriculum are outside the scope of her work. While it is understandable that she might wish to focus her discussion, why is it necessary to exclude schools completely from the definition of the field? This is an unnecessary division of the field. On the other side is Shifra Schonmann's charge that applied drama is 'stifling' and 'obstructing' drama education because of its disengagement with the theatrical aesthetic:

> My basic claim is that our young field, drama/theatre education, feels old because we do not challenge the aesthetic language. This is because we are stifled by applied drama and theatre that have so often put real obstacles in the way of broadening the horizon of the field by its expansion of the utilitarian function of theatre in the curriculum and beyond. (Schonmann, 2005, p. 38)

This divide is potentially damaging to the growth of both drama in education and applied theatre. While it is true that applied theatre has a rapid and to some quite bewildering rise, it has not to this point caused the kind of rifts we have experienced in drama education in the past. Rather than repeating the mistakes of the past, an approach that seeks mutual understanding and mutual growth is perhaps a more beneficial way forward. Using this approach, drama educators would identify themselves as applied theatre practitioners as well as drama educators without an implied hierarchy, leaving us free to give and receive the rich gifts of both fields.

As I see it, the field faces two major challenges. I think the first is to escape the already emerging tendency to push away from the drama education community that I would argue gave the field its initial methodology and impetus. Many of the pioneers in this area such as Judith Ackroyd, Bruce Burton and John O'Toole were grounded in drama education and they still work actively in both fields. It is true of course that the fields of theatre and performance studies are also crucial to the development of the area. We should as a community resist the tribalism that comes so naturally and endeavour to make the conversations cross the sometimes trivial boundaries that we create. To dichotomize this area now in at this stage of its development would be profoundly unwise. After all we have enough resistance to applied theatre and drama education without generating our own.

The history of drama education provides us with several clear indications of how and why the teaching of drama has developed in the way it has. This rich and sometimes complex history has left drama education with a viable and strong place within arts education. The next chapter locates drama within the arts and aesthetic education curriculum spaces.

Notes

1 David Hornbrook was an arts inspector for the London Burrough of Camden and Associate fellow of the Central School of Speech and Drama.

2 Gavin Bolton (1998), first used this term to describe the earliest drama practitioners and theorists. I use the term here with the realization that not all of the pioneers necessarily had a constructive influence on drama education.

3 Constantin Stanislavski (1863–1938), was famous for his work as a theatre director at the Moscow Arts Theatre and his 'method' actor training techniques (Hartnoll, 1985, p. 238).

4 Bertolt Brecht (1898–1956) was a German dramatist and director and co-founded the Berliner Ensemble. In his work he strove to make audience observe the epic nature of politics and history (Hartnoll, 1985, pp. 224–5).

5 It is true that Heathcote created jargon to explain her techniques such as Mantle of the Expert. It might be argued that this had the potential to mystify her followers and others as Hornbrook suggests.

6 Some may argue that there is perhaps a more subtle form of control going on in the teacher in role strategy.

7 John O'Toole claims that Norah Morgan was using this approach with Canadian Air Force officers in the 1940's (O'Toole et al., 2009, p. 103).

8 This editorial oversimplifies Bolton's contribution. The description here is by way of introduction to the partnership rather than seeking to ignore Bolton's significant practical contribution.

9 He later reconceptualizes this position (Bolton, 1998).

10 The term process drama was introduced by John O'Toole (1992).

11 I am not suggesting that Heathcote and Bolton encouraged the emergence of these dichotomies. To suggest that Heathcote was opposed to theatre or product is an oversimplification.

12 IDEA is the International Drama Theatre in Education Association.

13 Morgan and Saxton (1991) explore questioning techniques for teachers generally which draws on their practice and theoretical work as drama educators.

14 He is referring here metaphorically to other subjects that vie for attention in the curriculum.

15 Dorothy Heathcote identified these elements initially (Wagner, 1976, p. 147), Haseman and O'Toole organized and clarified their use for the classroom.

16 Forum theatre is a technique pioneered by Augusto Boal that asks the audience as to respond to a problem scene and resolve the underlying issue. In this approach audiences and actors are both spectators and actors, or what Boal calls 'spect-actors'.

4 Drama and Aesthetic Education

Aesthetic education: encounters with exploding cars

I was walking through a large modern art exhibition recently with my two young sons who were peering up at the most amazing installations. At this Bienalle were several astounding works including a series of cars suspended from the roof of a large turbine hall with light sticks emerging from them as if in an amazing and fantastic explosion in suspended animation. This installation in particular was quite arresting for the young and the old members of the audience. After the boys had spent slightly more than the usual 30 seconds (this is a high compliment to the artist concerned) considering the installation before running to the next one, they stopped and said: 'where can we do art, not just look at it'. I was tempted to give them the lecture that my elders had given me about art appreciation when it occurred to me that it wasn't just youthful impatience speaking, I was actually witnessing before my own eyes in my own family a shift in what young people understand as aesthetic education. What these young boys wanted was not only to appreciate the art form but also to actually engage with it themselves as participants – as audience and makers simultaneously. They wanted to make the exploding car sequence themselves.

This vignette demonstrates for me the responsibility we have as aesthetic educators to engage deeply with the art form as audience, and also to create bridges between the silos of making and appreciating. What my two young boys saw in the magnificence of Cai Guo-Qiang's work was the potential for their own creation if only they had access to the means and opportunity to make it. That in essence is what our role as aesthetic educators is all about; providing the means and the opportunity for young people not only to appreciate great works of art be they in a turbine hall, a theatre or an art gallery, but to use their innovation and creativity to create works of art themselves.

Aesthetic education: debunking some myths

For a reason that I cannot entirely grasp, aesthetics has been shrouded with a kind of mysterious aura. Perhaps the mystery is motivated by some artists who want to control knowledge about the arts and hide knowledge about artistic practice. Whatever the case and whoever the culprits, there is little to be gained by mystifying artistic practice and aesthetic education. The teacher's role is the exact opposite to mystification; it is to make the mysterious knowable, but more than knowable; it is to create a structured understanding of, in this case, aesthetics and to allow students to use that aesthetic to create their own work. Rather than holding the knowledge in some pointless power play, we are handing it over to the next generation to re-infuse it with their own innovative powers and change this generation's aesthetics beyond our recognition or imagination. So in the end drama education is aesthetic education as it provides access to knowledge about the forms and structures of the art form that will assure its continued relevance and dynamism.

Defining aesthetics

There have been some insightful and useful books on the ins and outs of defining what the aesthetic might mean. I could devote the rest of the book to this argument alone, but I have chosen instead to settle on a recent curriculum definition that I think suits drama education. According to the Australian Curriculum, Assessment and Reporting Authority (2010, p. 26), 'Aesthetic describes the fusion of our thoughts, senses and emotions with the diversity of our personal, social and imagined experience which comprises our response to artworks'. What is slightly under-recognized in this definition is that our response to artworks might be in the creation of them ourselves, so our ability to control aesthetics relies on these responses; in short, you need to know about drama (including its processes, forms etc) to make and perform drama.

Drama and aesthetic education

As discussed in the previous chapter, the short but occasionally stormy history of drama education has discussed *ad nauseum* the tension between process and product. For me and for many others this is a fairly pointless argument. We are aesthetic educators and as such we engage with the aesthetics of our art form to help the young people we teach connect with the art form, to understand it, and ultimately we hope the world around them more. But understanding is only the first step; giving young people access to the tools of creation in drama is essential if we want them to reach their potential as creators of drama. Perhaps drama educators have a special responsibility because like dance educators, we focus on the body and the mind being the essential tools of creation. There are no instruments to acquire and no materials to shape. Often it is just the physical body in the empty space that is essential to our art form. While educators should always seek to make processes and approaches known to their students, I am not arguing here for an art form that is devoid of wonder and mystery; actually quite the opposite. The paradox here is the more we demystify the processes of creation, the more able will our students be to create the mysterious. Unlike the magician whose powers depend on the secrets of the trade for audience engagement, theatre relies on the audience's willing suspension of disbelief to draw them into the mysteries, absurdities and the wonder of live performance. Giving students access to that knowledge, skills and understanding will allow new generations to create theatre full of questions, mystery and meaning.

Aesthetic education and beauty

Prominent drama educator Joe Winston has recently re-energized a discussion around the place of beauty in education. His argument is that educational philosophers have long considered beauty a core educational value (Winston, 2010, p. 72) and an antidote to much of the mechanistic and reductive teaching that currently exists. He argues: 'If more teachers can come to recognize that beauty matters to them, that it can re-energize, rehumanize, and remoralize their practice, then its re-articulation in educational discourse might begin to counter the more pernicious and reductive effects of technicist thinking' (Winston, 2010, p. 85).

Winston's argument is persuasive. He manages to engage with a basic tenet of our existence in a way that does not romanticize beauty, but rather positions it as a central feature of an education that makes all the participants feel fully human. He argues that the potential interaction of beauty and play in the drama classroom present a unique opportunity: 'Drama as a curriculum practice provides a particular kind of play space for a particular kind of social play, one where, unlike sport, there need be no winners or losers and no one need get physically hurt . . . . In drama, beauty operates within two dimensions – the social and the artistic – which jointly frame the ways in which teachers and students have to work' (Winston, 2010, p. 83).

A repositioning of beauty at the centre of education implies some profound shifts in teaching practice. It means that teachers will need to spend time identifying beauty and then structuring and scaffolding approaches that make it a feature of classroom learning. While some may see this as a way of engaging in a high art versus low art discussion, this approach should be rejected as needlessly divisive. Happily Winston in his discussion of beauty does not buy into this binary. In his recent book *Beauty and Education* (2010), he discusses instances of the beautiful in what some (though not Winston) might define as high and low culture. For him, beauty is discoverable in the so-called refined and the popular, in the works of Shakespeare and the songs of Bob Dylan. Art critic John Carey argues that the low art/high art divide is 'unverifiable and meaningless' (2006, p. 32) and is more a function of intellectual snobbery than any serious engagement with arts practice, let alone teaching. Much in modern culture validates this argument. The film industry is one of the sites where the cultural divide has narrowed. Quentin Tarantino who was jealously claimed as a high cinema artist is not only thoroughly popular; he traces many of his influences to popular culture. Tarantino's bridging of the low culture /high culture divide is a product of his approach to his audience. He says of them: 'I don't believe in elitism. I don't think the audience is this dumb person lower than me. I am the audience' (Herschberg, 1997, p. 116).

Joe Winston's call for teachers to embrace beauty is timely. In a world where the testing of technical quantifiable knowledge is overwhelming schools and schooling, the call for drama teachers to fight the rising tide with an understanding and appreciation of beauty is deeply provocative. It stands in opposition to much that our current systems embrace. The question for teachers is how this might be possible. In the next section of this chapter, I would like to turn to a model of aesthetic education (which is incidentally not the same as an education about beauty in my view) that allows for teaching that reveals much about beauty and what it is to be a citizen of the twenty-first century.

A unified model of drama learning and teaching

If we are to honour the desire of our young people not only to be appreciators but to be makers of art, a model of learning is required that effectively integrates the essentials of learning processes in appreciating and making without siloing them off as binaries. Instead the model proposed here conceptualizes learning drama as an interactive and mutually dependant process. The model was generated (Anderson and Jefferson, 2009) when I (with my co-author Miranda Jefferson) were conceptualizing film learning situated within arts

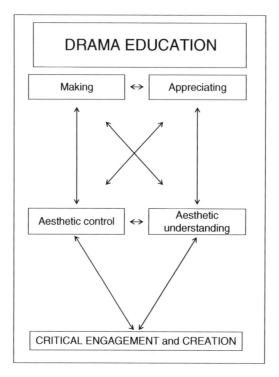

Figure 4.1 Pedagogy for aesthetic education in drama

education. What we have discovered since is that teachers across the arts find this model useful to describe the way learning can work in the arts.

In this model, appreciation and making are interdependent processes that continually promote and sustain the other in drama learning. The aesthetics of the art form are not shadowy and mysterious; rather the control and understanding of them form the basis of learning in drama. The interdependency creates an unbroken relationship between the understanding of the art form through appreciation and the creation of that art form. Or to put it another way, understanding in drama comes from knowing and doing and sometimes that occurs at the same time. An example of this process is illustrated by a recent theatrical adaptation of Guus Kuijer's (2006) award winning children's tale *The Book of Everything.* In the play, we meet the young child Thomas Klopper who introduces his family to the audience and finally we meet his repressive and violent father. Without going into too much of the plot there is a scene in the play where the plagues of Egypt are being visited upon the father in Thomas' imagination. This is created in the theatre when the audience is given ping pong balls and asked to throw them at the stage on cue. They do so enthusiastically and the stage is inundated with frogs (ping pong balls). All of the audience know that they are just ping pong balls, even the five-year-old children, but it creates an important piece of theatrical understanding about the willing suspension of disbelief that is essential to meaning being created for the audience. The symbolism of the frogs is created and executed by using a simple yet powerful device. If this moment of theatrical understanding is moved to the students' own making processes in drama, they can realize that creating the illusion, for instance a plague of frogs, does not actually require any frogs at all. In their work they can call on symbolism and the willing suspension of disbelief to powerfully use the aesthetic to create dramatic meaning. The understanding is fully realized only when the appreciation is transformed into creation through the drama making process. I would like to reflect on the elements of the model now to further develop the discussion of the place of the aesthetic in drama education.

Appreciating drama: interactive engagement

Appreciation has perhaps been derided a little in recent times in arts education. By appreciation I mean the educative process where students analyse drama as performance. This entails drama of all kinds including professional performances, performances of their peers and even observation of the performative in everyday life. This moves beyond personal preferences to engage in a deeper way with qualities of performances.

Appreciation is sometimes called 'critically studying', 'responding' or 'apprehending' but most of these terms refer to the same process of being an audience to a performance (Hughes, 2007, p. 601). Or perhaps more realistically as O'Toole et al. (2009) put it: 'Young people are taught to appreciate drama primarily as consumers, both for its supposed civilizing influence and to generate audience for adult theatre' (2009, p. 129). Schonman (2007, p. 587) argues that Brecht '. . . challenges the conventional relationship between the stage and the audience looking to the political influence of theatre and the political commitment of an audience'. Rather than appreciation just being a matter of personal taste, in drama it is an engagement with the social, political and historical elements of human existence. Augusto Boal takes this approach one step further by blurring the line between the actor and the audience creating the 'spect-actor' where the roles of the actor and the spectator are fused to allow the audience to live within the action and hence the implications of the drama. The interdependence of making and appreciation are bound up in this one process.

Boal's approach is also instructive for educators. The audience need no longer sit more or less quietly as they are subjected to theatre, they can in effect engage in the event as active participants. So Boal and also Brecht's take on appreciation is that it is an active process intellectually (for Brecht) and physically (for Boal). This approach is ideally suited to the demands of modern drama classrooms. It allows for audience, not only to appreciate, but critique and intervene in the work when necessary. In practice, this changes the traditional role of students as audience sitting in rows watching work.

In a recent drama class I was teaching, some students were showing works in progress. Armed with their understanding of the elements of drama (Haseman and O'Toole, 1986), I asked them to walk around the performance space and stop the performers during the work if they wanted to make a critique of the process. At first students felt a little uncomfortable engaging with performance in this way. It is, after all, a radical departure from what they have been told an audience should do. After some time, getting acclimatized to the new approach and with some interventions and support from me (the teacher), the audience became active in the making process through the critical feedback for the performers.

Performance theorist Baz Kershaw goes further calling upon the audience to become 'radical spectators' (1994) and 'unruly audience' (2001). Certainly the work of theatre companies such as Blast Theory, Le Fura Del Baus and Welfare State International not only make this approach possible, but sometimes they downright demand it of their audience. In response to Kershaw's provocation, Monica Prendegast (2008) asks logical questions such as: 'What does a radical spectator look like? How does this spectator resist the commodification and consumerism of performance? How does this kind of spectator encounter and engage with performance?'

What Kershaw is calling for in an audience may not be feasible in the classroom, but it does lay the groundwork for a more interactive experience that will be more familiar to a twenty-first-century audience. I am not suggesting here a disrespectful parody of Elizabethan audience interactions (cue insults and hurling of rotten fruit and vegetables). I do think Kershaw's call for less passivity in the audience is complementary to the demands of a modern drama classroom where appreciating and making are interdependent.

Activating the audience in this way is not new. Boal's Forum Theatre and even side-coaching approaches from TheatreSports feature these kinds of interactions. Engaging the audience in this way allows audiences a more central role in the aesthetics of the work. It metaphorically allows them to get their hands on the motor of the drama and tune the work as a mechanic would. In terms of theatrical practice, it positions the audience as directors, allowing them to be in the middle of the aesthetic development of the work rather than the passive appreciating audience that theatregoers have become in many Western theatres. This approach also overcomes much that is problematic about appreciation in drama. Schonmann (2007, p. 597) calls appreciation the 'missing link' in drama education. She argues: 'Appreciating theatre and enjoying theatre are active processes that develop the abilities to grasp questions of application, generalization and symbolism'. In concert with critically and aesthetically aware audiences, we need to make our students theatre makers, who bring their appreciating skills and knowledge to the drama creation process.

Making and performing drama

Another significant component of the model will be well known to most drama teachers. It is what is variously described as making, performing, devising, generating or composing etc. Many drama educators and drama syllabuses actually differentiate the making from the performing of the process and although there may be some point to doing this, it seems to be part of the same continuum. When students are making work, be it from an existing script such as *The Laramie Project* or devising their own process, they are always in the process of making something for performance. The point of associating making and performing so closely is that live dramatic performance is always in a constant process of being made and remade. Each performance of a work is by the nature of the interaction with the audience different in subtle and sometimes not so subtle ways. Thus, while there is obviously a difference in the processes of making and performing drama, it is part of the same process. This is quite different from what happens in film for instance, where the product is more or less fixed and films are 'exhibited' or 'shown' as opposed to plays that are 'performed'.

Critiques of making: the devising process examined

The making and devising process is a ubiquitous part of drama learning the world over. The approach in drama classrooms has not, however, been without criticism. David Hornbrook argued:

> Ever since Peter Slade first *asked* children to 'find a space', students in drama classrooms all over the world have *been asked to get into small groups* and improvise dramas. The devised improvisation remains *overwhelmingly the predominant modus operandi* of the drama class: satisfying as it does so many of the field's precepts, it has become, over the years, simply the natural way of doing things. *Yet for all its* popularity, the devised improvisation, seen in the context of world drama, is a very unusual form indeed. Having no writer, no script, no director, no stage manager (everyone, in theory, does everything), it is uniquely *undifferentiated in its production.* Then, although it is also likely to be *about* something in a big way – racism, homelessness, drugs (the *result* of the influence of the 'issue' in classroom drama), it will also, paradoxically, for all the gravity of its subject matter, be short; usually no more than twenty minutes or so and sometimes considerably less. *And finally, and most significantly for my argument here*, it may be successfully created by a group of students who have never done drama before or who have developed no particular theatrical skills. *It cannot be said that these* conditions remotely characterize theatre production anywhere else. (1989, p. 55)

I have quoted David Hornbrook at length here because I think this critique of common practice, while in many ways flawed, raises some important criticisms of making in drama classrooms. David Hornbrook's contribution to the discussions about drama learning and teaching has ensured that drama education has not drifted so that it is virtually unrecognizable from the art form that it reflects. To be fair, he is commenting on practice that is more reflective of last century than this century. Helen Nicholson maintains that Hornbrook '. . . challenged the orthodoxies of drama-in-education, arguing that its roots in progressive education and its emphasis on spontaneous improvisation militated against young people learning theatre as an art form' (2009, p. 38). His impetus helped drama swing the pendulum back a little closer to the aesthetics of theatre, but his critique overreaches in some distinct but crucial ways. The first way he overreaches is to assume that professional theatre is the ultimate model for drama learning.

Schools are not theatres

As I discussed earlier, schools are not and never should be theatres in the same way that they should not be stock markets or mechanics workshops or even artists' studios. These spaces are qualitatively different from schools for a good reason. Drama education is not first and foremost about the art form; it is about the student. While many of the practices of the stock market, artist's studio or garage might make sense for that context, they are potentially less useful for schools. If we accept that premise, then it follows that drama education, rather than being a facsimile of the theatre, will draw from the aesthetics of the art form in a dynamic way to establish, sustain and nurture its practice. In the same way drama education in most places is not primarily to train actors, directors or any other kind of theatre worker. It is to provide students with a way of understanding themselves and the world around them. While many students do go on to work in the theatre, most will never 'tread the boards' or take any other role apart from that of an audience in professional theatre. Is this concerning? Not really; do you hear many history teachers concerned by the lack of professional historians coming out of high school history? In the end, we allow students an insight into how they can engage with the art form to learn about that aesthetic in its own right, but perhaps more importantly to understand the world and how they might negotiate it.

Poor practice does not constitute standard practice

The second flaw is the assumption that poor practice is standard practice. His claim that work can be created by those who have never done drama before does not accurately reflect what happens in the continuum of drama learning. Julie Dunn (2003) persuasively argues that even from the early years of schooling, young people engage with taking on roles and dramatic play. This, like any area of education, grows and changes as they learn how to change play into more structured forms that more closely reflect theatrical practice. The work Hornbrook is critiquing is based on this learning which, while perhaps tacit, is still present. Effective and perceptive drama teachers engage their students and promote their development using these foundations, but just as crucially draw on the dynamic aesthetic of the theatre. Of course there are some teachers who run rambling and formless improvisations on random social issues, but that does not represent effective practice.

Devised drama is unusual in world drama

His argument that devised drama is a very 'unusual form indeed' will come as somewhat of a shock to theatre makers whose stock in trade is group devised work. I am thinking here of Welfare State International, Mike Leigh, Blast Theory, Version 1.0, Theatre de Complicite who rely in their work to some extent on ensemble devising processes. Complicite describe themselves on their website as 'a constantly evolving ensemble of performers and collaborators . . . Complicite is more than a theatre company: it is a state of mind. When each collaborative adventure into the unknown starts off, anything is possible. The result is an astonishingly broad and continually evolving spectrum of work' (sourced from *Theatre de* Complicite website at www.complicite.org/about/ on 29 November 2010). Missing from these companies are the flagship national and international theatres, but closer inspection reveals that the development arms of these flagship companies have intensive and dynamic ensemble devising work in production. So to say this work is 'unusual' was an overstatement even in 1989.

Devised drama is undifferentiated in its production roles

The improvisation that Hornbrook imagines is an unstructured free for all that does not draw from or respect the various theatrical roles that bring works of drama to life. While there are some unstructured experiences in the drama classroom that are worthwhile, it is a rare drama classroom today where this is only the case. Most drama classrooms use improvisation alongside developing works from published scripts, exploring forms of world theatre from Aeschylus to Edward Albee. A feature of this learning is the development of skills in the very roles Hornbrook argues are lacking: playwriting, direction, design and so on. While there will also be a place for drama that examines and explores through process alone, very few classrooms relinquish the power of the process of making drama in all its forms.

Devised drama deals with big issues very briefly

Here I think Hornbrook has a strong argument. One of the enduring issues of classroom drama work in my experience is the tendency for drama teachers and students to drive epic themes into small performances. While the work of Brecht and Boal (to some extent) demonstrate it is possible to examine the epic with modest resources, they do so over an extended period for the most part. As I mentioned earlier, the drama classroom is not the same as a theatre and younger students are not often capable of working in those same ways.

As an external examiner of senior drama work, I think I have probably seen over 1000 group-devised performances over about 15 years. One of the conclusions I can draw from seeing so many performances is that this kind of drama is a genre all of its own with few parallels in theatre generally. To that extent Hornbrook is right. But so what? If we accept that theatre and schools do not necessarily need to be the same and that drama education can draw from the aesthetics of theatre, it is completely valid for schools to create a drama form that meets the needs and capabilities of students. The best of this kind of theatre draws from the aesthetics of theatre to create a clear and dramatically meaningful performance. Some of the time, that is about big themes and ideas but often it is just a premise, an idea, a musing or an impression, like theatre more generally.

Devised drama, when taught effectively, draws from the aesthetics of theatre. These aesthetics are 'taught not caught' and rely on learning that explicitly engages with aesthetic control and aesthetic understanding.

Aesthetic control and aesthetic understanding

If we agree that providing access to the rules and principles of the art form has merit, we must then decide how this can occur in drama learning. The dual concepts of aesthetic control and aesthetic understanding are interdependent concepts that are integral to drama learning. Aesthetic control describes the choices made in the drama.

Aesthetic control

Aesthetic control is central to the way students engage with drama and in fact, any art form. The concept arose from the need to describe how learners can engage with the aesthetic processes of drama, but also to suggest this is a skill that increases with learning and experience. For instance, if you watch a 12-year-old student attempting a Shakespearean character for the first time, there is a tendency for an exaggerated delivery. In my experience, young people often mistake extroversion for acting. As the student's skills and experience develop, the actor learns when to use subtlety and nuance rather than excessive of sound and movement. In this development, the student is growing in aesthetic control. In essence, the beginning actor is developing an understanding of the craft of acting, but also controlling the aesthetic processes that make the art form effective. The elements of drama are in large part an attempt to map some of the aesthetics of drama. The concept of aesthetic control works across all learning in drama including the skills of the playwright, director designer and so on. In these roles aesthetic control cannot exist without an interaction with aesthetic understanding.

Aesthetic understanding

In the model and in classroom drama practice, aesthetic understanding is the descendent of appreciating although it is not appreciation in the passive, distant sense. Aesthetic understanding is only achieved where students engage in the aesthetic and begin learning about the control of drama. Understanding (which is different from knowledge) in the drama classroom allows students to engage with dramatic process and product from the inside, to tinker with it, to tune it and to refine the art form. Understanding here is not passive; it is rather informed by the knowledge of the practitioner. Much of the knowledge within drama is tacit, that is, it is only understood through an embodied experience. It is understood innately, instinctively by the actor, the playwright and the designer. This tacit knowledge is often only accessible through the experience of the art form. David Wright whose research focuses on embodiment in the drama classroom reflects on the complex interactions taking place: He says: '"It" [drama learning] arises in the complex feedback systems that comprise communication between mind(s) and body(ies). It is a consequence of the recursive processes of reflection and improvisation. These processes can generate challenging and unpredictable results' (2005, p. 1).

The complex interchange of feedback systems according to Wright (2005) facilitates learning through a recursive mind/body active/reflective cycle. Understanding is not conceptualized as a simple cognition; rather it is a more complex interaction between the body and the mind to create understanding. This is a substantial challenge for drama teachers. The complexity of learning here is fairly unique and countercultural in schooling systems that elevate knowledge above action and experience. In short, aesthetic understanding in drama can only be achieved when the body and the mind are engaged. This does not mean that our students should stop being an audience. Quite the contrary, in my experience, they become more engaged and a more analytically astute audience when they understand the drama as a spectator and an actor. These expanded perspectives move beyond the superficial understandings (facts about characters, the themes of the play) to a deeper engagement with the dramatic meaning of a performance and how that dramatic meaning is created. The engine metaphor might be useful here again. I know the facts about the internal combustion engine, I know about the pistons and the fuel and I even have a fair understanding about how my car impacts on the environment. I do not however know it like my mechanic does. He understands my engine because he has worked on it, tuned it and refined it over many years. He understands it from the inside out because he has experience working with it. In this analogy, students who have not worked with drama (the engine) cannot know it as well as those who have actually worked on it. Given the complex understanding and often embodiment required in drama, it is simply not possible to understand it fully without working from within it. If the processes of aesthetic control and aesthetic understanding are intertwined, it provides the optimum conditions for critical engagement and creation to emerge in drama learning.

Critical engagement and creation

The process of drama learning described here culminates in the union of critical engagement and creation. By critical I mean the application of informed and careful judgement when engaging with drama and creating drama. Beyond making and appreciating, these terms deliberately blur the edges of the two processes. Students of drama can be in the process of creation as they are reflecting on drama, and they can create drama as they are appreciating drama. They are intersecting domains of the dramatic process and the overlap at this point should be so comprehensive that engagement and creation may look like identical processes at times.

The crucial element of this final piece of the model is the application of judgement. This judgement is born of the developing aesthetic understanding and control. Thus for instance, when a student is watching a performance of *Mother Courage,* she should be able to engage with the work understanding it from the inside as a performer because she has worked on

Brechtian theatrical techniques herself as a performance maker. She should also be able to make judgements about the work from a critical perspective based on her aesthetic understanding which incorporates the ways the social and historical context have been incorporated into the development of meaning in the work. This in turn will allow the student to create her own Brechtian performance (critical creation) using her developing aesthetic control understanding the social and historical context and create a performance (critical creation) that carries that social and historical meaning. This model is aspirational as all models in education are. In the next few chapters, we will discuss how the realities of the drama classroom allow for and sometimes prevent these lofty aspirations being fulfilled.

Conclusions

The drama classroom is an aesthetic laboratory like no other. It is not the same as the theatre and it is not the same as other classrooms, even other arts classrooms. It is a place where young people can explore the human condition by drawing on the wellspring of theatrical form and devices. It is a place where their own work can and should bump shoulders with William Shakespeare, Caryl Churchill, Edward Bond, Federico García Lorca and Tracy Letts. This approach demands a pedagogy that builds understanding of dramatic form from the inside rather than as a distant audience member. The implication for teaching and in a sense what the dramatic aesthetic demands is a classroom where students know through immersion in the creative processes themselves. The model of aesthetic learning proposed here provides one approach in the ongoing evolution of our pedagogy. A central part of this pedagogy is the teaching of collaborative learning that I will discuss in the next chapter.

Collaborative Understanding: Ensemble Approaches in Drama Education

5

Chapter Outline

The scene is pretty typical of drama education classrooms around the world. All my students are working on their own self-devised performances together. On one side of the room a group of solid rugby playing boys and self-conscious girls are giggling as they put on makeup (military war paint) and roll around the floor pretending to create a battle scene. In another area of the room, some of my more 'cerebral' students are discussing how to create distance between themselves and the audience to create a 'Brechtian distancing effect so that the audience won't concentrate on our characters but on our message'. Other groups are bickering, some quite loudly about what they want to do but all of them are learning to a large extent about drama but also about life, about negotiating relationships, about negotiating their own identity, about who they are and how they would like others to perceive them. As Peter O'Connor says: 'All drama learning is about how to act. It would be a very limited view of drama education to suggest this is only about acting on stage. A wider view is that in drama in education students learn how to be actors in the real world' (O'Connor, 2010, p. xxiii). Perhaps this scene is so commonplace for drama educators we forget that at its base is something radical: teachers leading by facilitating students as they collaborate and work together to create drama.

In very few classrooms are students entrusted to negotiate their own learning together. This radical creative collaboration is a hallmark of dynamic drama education that we rarely allow ourselves to celebrate; but it is for many students the only place where they can communicate the idea and issues that are meaningful to them and their peers in creative ways.

You may have noticed that I have not described my role as teacher in this part of the classroom narrative. I am part of the back-story. The entire drama staff in this particular school has worked with these students for years, teaching them about the processes that make this kind of collaborative creation possible. We have taught them about group devising from the work of Allison Oddey and improvisation through the work of Viola Spolin and Keith Johnstone, and through Brecht's epic theatre how audiences might be engaged with the drama but enjoy enough distance to understand the politics of the scene. This is not a 'set and forget' class I am describing; on the contrary, the collaborative making process has been deliberately taught to make this classroom possible.

This chapter examines how collaboration is and should be at the heart of learning and teaching programs in drama education. It looks at some of the relevant educational theory and research to support the ensemble approach to learning that is at the heart of so much drama education. The chapter details five principles for creating a viable community of learners in drama who can engage effectively in drama learning.

Learning to play with the aesthetic . . . together

We have discussed Henry Caldwell Cook's contribution to drama earlier. His approach that prized collaboration made him a drama pioneer (Bolton, 1998). His contribution was to place collaboration at the centre of his classroom practice (Watson, 2008). His exhortation of his students to 'act it' (Caldwell Cook, 1917, p. 272) was and sadly still is in stark contrast to the moribund text-only approaches to the performing arts still found in many classrooms that feature individual desk-bound quiet study over collaborative learning.

His approach to collaboration is similar to that practised in contemporary classrooms. The differences lie in his reliance on the classics and his understatement of self-devising in his classroom work. Of student devised work, he is deeply concerned about the disasters that may ensue (Caldwell Cook, 1917, p. 272). While he prefers the classics as a base, he prescribes play as a way to begin work. He describes his classroom:

> Some sit at the desks while others stand before them or lean over their shoulders. They [the students] are gathered in working groups, putting their brown heads together for the making of their play; and the room is full of an industrious chatter. A visitor entering suddenly might fancy that he had come by mistake into a classroom of the old school in the absence of the master; for the noise of allowed play sounds at first just like the noise of disorder. But if you listen, you will find it is articulate. (Caldwell Cook, 1917, p. 302)

Caldwell Cook's legacy to drama education is the legitimization of imaginative, collaborative and experimental play. While many educators recognize this is a mandatory precursor to creativity, Caldwell Cook through his employment of the 'double meaning' of play is inviting his students to engage with the aesthetic in a playful way. This differs from Way whose development through drama approach (discussed in Chapter Three) removed the aesthetic dimension and sought to eliminate formic boundaries to allow students unfettered creative freedom. In Caldwell Cook's approach, the aesthetic creates a set of guides or scaffolds for students to work within and allows them the freedom to explore actively the art form. David Hornbrook criticizes Caldwell Cook's practice as an 'idiosyncratic Boys Own Paper . . .' style that reflects the 'heady progressivism' of the day (1989, p. 7). What Hornbrook fails to recognize is the uniqueness of the blending of the relatively rigid formic conventions of the dramatic aesthetic with one of the first experiential and collaborative classrooms.

Foundations of ensemble education: sociocultural approaches to learning

A student's development, Vygotsky argues, is informed by a dynamic threshold of what the student is capable of learning through interaction with others, rather than the capability of what they can already achieve alone. In other words, students develop and learn more when 'they all put their minds together'. Vygotsky describes this dynamic threshold or ready potential in students as the zone of proximal development. He explains it as '. . . the distance between the actual development level as determined by independent problem solving and the level of potential development as determined through problem solving under adult supervision or in collaboration with more capable peers' (1978, p. 86).

Vygotsky likens students' internalized learning in the zone of proximal development to 'buds' of the 'flowers' of development, rather than the 'fruits' of development. If a student can successfully complete a task alone, then according to Vygotsky, there is no longer a zone of proximal development but the attainment of the actual development level. Therefore, '. . . learning which is oriented toward developmental levels that have already been reached is ineffective from the viewpoint of a child's overall development' (1978, p. 89).

In Vygotskian terms, the process of social interaction with other students serves to internalize the learning. He says that '. . . learning awakens a variety of internal developmental processes that are able to operate only when the child is interacting with people in his environment and in cooperation with his peers. Once these processes are internalized, they become part of the child's independent development achievement' (1978, p. 90).

In the classroom, the dynamic of social interaction (group work) within a sequenced learning structure (scaffolding) puts the students learning process ahead of the student's developmental process. Teaching then is leading a student's development, rather than responding to it. The idea is that this is achieved by (1) organizing social interactions in the classroom between students in problem solving tasks with teacher assistance, and (2) designing a sequenced learning structure that 'provides the basis for the subsequent development of a variety of highly complex internal processes in children's thinking' (1978, p. 90). Scaffolded learning in drama fulfils Vygotsky's principles and the characteristics of collaborative learning.

Aesthetics, collaboration and engagement

An arts way of learning is rooted in the idea that the experience of learning is combined with the experience of an aesthetic. The learning involves feelings and understandings of the world that are heightened, refined and rendered more subtle and complex through the aesthetic of the arts (Eisner, 2002). The learning in arts education is defined not only by having an experience with *art works*; it is more significantly in the experience of *working with* and *in* the art. The experience of the aesthetic through *working* is central to the drama pedagogy with its focus on *process* as a means of learning. What is obvious to drama educators (Heathcote, 1991; O'Neill, 1995; Bowell and Heap, 2001) is that valuable cognitive learning happens when students engage with the subtle and challenging process of working together to negotiate and make dramatic meaning. The same is apparent in the *process* of making drama.

The *process* of drama learning involves students through embodiment and enactment, focusing, imagining, creating, investigating, reflecting, problem-solving, collaborating and communicating (Bowell and Heap, 2001). Collaborative practice in particular is integral to drama making and performing, and a fundamental underpinning of the drama pedagogy as a model of social learning theory (Dewey, 1938; Bruner, 1977; Vygotsky, 1978).

The role of the teacher in collaborative drama learning

Providing a scaffolded learning framework and organized group work requires active teacher facilitation in drama. The teacher must have knowledge of the students and a deep knowledge the aesthetics of theatre and drama pedagogy. If optimal learning occurs in Vygotsky's proximal zone of development, students require the teacher to learn and be guided in scaffolded and collaborative learning. The idea is that students are taught fundamental understandings in an area of learning and explore and consolidate these understandings through challenging task-oriented group work. The teacher leads students to develop their cognitive abilities by allowing them in groups to explore, experiment and solve problems. In short, as students create drama they are attempting to create, control and communicate by using specific elements of the dramatic aesthetic in collaboration with each other. The teaching scaffold is the instructional support that the teacher creates for the students to embark on these approaching tasks. The challenge in teaching is in providing a learning experience through tasks that are demanding, but achievable for students. Both collaborative and creative work challenges and consolidates student learning because the students in group work have to take mutual responsibility for their learning. Teachers in a collaborative learning environment must participate in this mutual responsibility for student learning as well. Collaboration in itself is a process that teachers have to actively teach.

Learning to collaborate

Devising in student groups needs to be a valued enterprise for all the participants. Devising drama means students must actively engage with each other for creation to work and when active engagement occurs; the experience is like the transcendental experience that Eisner (2002) describes as inherent not only in the product of the art's aesthetic but also in its process. Students engaged in the processes that I described at the opening of this chapter require sustained concentration and more than a little skill in negotiating interpersonal interactions.

A teacher managing student group devising work requires the same skills as students need to collaborate effectively in a group. Both teachers and students have to listen, communicate, share, negotiate, encourage, organize and have mutual responsibility to achieve a common goal in learning. This is near impossible to achieve if students haven't developed these skills. The only way the students will collaborate well is if collaborating is actively taught as part of their learning. Trust, listening and the ability to take risks are integral for the success of collaboration and creativity. Drama teachers actively develop this social culture of working through their experiential and creative activities and tasks in the classroom. Helen Nicholson argues that scaffolded drama learning helps students to 'recognize the implications of the task and, crucially for the establishment of trust, why they have been asked to work in these ways (2002, p. 85). When students recognize the value of collaborating in their shared enterprise or task, they develop a culture of mutual trust.

Trust in the collaborative learning environment of drama is related directly to the concept of risk-taking and creative experimentation. They are the seeds for discovery learning (Bruner, 1977) and meeting the challenges of the zone of proximal development (Vygotsky, 1978). Nicholson explains how trust, debate and experimentation need to be inculcated in the drama classroom. She says: 'In relation to drama education, a productive and creative environment built on an ethic of care does not mean that there will be agreement between participants; on the contrary, a political theory of trust acknowledges that a caring environment may create a robust environment in which debate, dissent, generosity and artistic experimentation might be encouraged and valued' (2002, p. 90).

John O'Toole explains how the functions of playwright, performer, audience and director in Western theatre are performed by separate people with discrete tasks and responsibilities, but that in drama education these 'functions are subsumed in other functions and roles and another network of relationships – the real roles and purposes of people in school' (1992,

p. 4). In the drama classroom, for example, students creating drama through improvisation together are all performers, playwrights, directors and audience simultaneously.

The capacity and recognition of theatre as a collaborative art form describes drama pedagogical practices and concepts of shared roles in the creation of the live dramatic form. At the forefront of drama learning processes is experiential 'doing' or 'making' learning where ideas and skills are explored through communication, negotiation and collaboration between students in small groups or whole class groups. The process of communal collaboration in drama education is learning that is valued in itself as well as being the main conduit for other learning in drama. Drama in education does not dismiss the creative force of the director in theatre practice, but pedagogically in the classroom, drama learning involves students in group collaborative learning, coming together as shared participant creators of the drama. They do this by negotiating and exchanging ideas and roles to create, explore, challenge and solve.

Ensemble learning, collaborative understanding

Developing ensemble learning is not only practically vital for a drama classroom; it is really the DNA of drama pedagogy. If we strip drama back to fact-based learning about for example theatre history or how theatrical lights work, we are dispossessing young people of what Neelands calls the pro-social nature of drama education. Pro-social classrooms create a '. . . community and a common culture. Young people are beginning to model the conditions for a future society based in the necessity of learning how to live with the grave importance of our interdependence as humans . . .' (2009, p. 175). He argues that these kinds of classrooms model life. He describes these learning spaces: '. . . children and young people have been led to imagine and look for new ways of living together rather than against each other; to find solidarity in their common disadvantage; to create new models of pluralist community' (2009, p. 176).

While the facts and mechanics of drama are and will continue to be central to drama learning, it is the pro-social aspects of drama learning that make it an essential pedagogy for young people navigating their way in an increasingly complex world. Perhaps all pedagogies are pro-social in some respects, but drama in particular and the arts in general engage the participant in the dynamics of living; identity formation, negotiating relationships and collaborating to make and create shared imaginings. Jonathan Neelands argues: 'Working together in the social and egalitarian conditions of ensemble-based drama, young people have the opportunity to struggle with the demands of becoming a self-managing, self-governing, self-regulating social group who co-create artistically and socially and begin to model these . . . beyond their classrooms' (2009, p. 182).

Heathcote's advocacy for better learning, not better dramatics, in the well known *Signs and Portents* (Heathcote, 1984, p. 169) article is a call for a radical change in learning to make all curriculum pro-social. My own research and classroom practice and Jonothan Neelands' research in the area brings me back to the realization that effective drama learning is the best site of pro-social learning. Drama classrooms are researched as an environment for democracy, agency and identity because the conditions make them conducive to pro-social learning. So there is something precious here, something that should be the entitlement of each young person in our schools. In my view, this is the strongest argument for making drama the central of the curriculum around which pro-social learning could be created to meet the needs of this century and, not as schooling currently does, meeting the needs of schooling from the nineteenth century. Neelands explains why understanding of drama processes goes hand in hand with the understanding of the dramatic symbolic languages of theatre and hence society:

> Access and belonging to the culture of power requires knowledge of its symbolic and cultural heritage, sometimes referred to as 'cultural capital' and this can be acquired if it is made universally available through education that is the positive in the 'cultural offer' proposals. For some children, engagement with and access to the cultural learning associated with the culture of power is by accident of birth into the culture of power itself; most will rely on the vagaries of schooling which may or may not introduce them to the culture of the culture of power. In terms of power, all cultures are not equal. (Neelands, 2008, p. 10)

Which raises the question how do teachers provide those with low stocks of cultural capital access to the capital and how do we promote acceptance, tolerance and collaborative community making to those with high stocks of cultural capital in our classrooms?

Collaborative drama and intercultural learning

One change that is evident in our classrooms is the cultural religious and ethnic diversity of students, and to a lesser extent colleagues. I have included a discussion of intercultural learning here because it is a major learning opportunity for students in drama. In the act of negotiating identity and collaborating through creative dramatic processes, students have the opportunity to reflect and respond to a range of perspectives different from their own.

This ethnic diversity, which is a hallmark of modern cosmopolitan Western nations, is often in political and educational discussion positioned as a 'problem'. For the drama classroom, this difference provides untold potential for new insights and new understandings. Matthew Clausen is an Australian classroom-based drama researcher. His work to date has focussed on how his students can authentically engage with cultural diversity in the classroom. His most recent research saw him examining Indigenous Australian playtexts with a predominantly monocultural (Anglo Saxon) group of students. The following is Matthew Clausen's account of this work (Clausen, 2008).

Collaborative learning for Intercultural understanding in White classrooms: Matthew Clausen's experience

The term intercultural is the 'mixing' of ideas, traditions, beliefs, behaviours and values. It involves the individual's experience of other cultures, their conventions, beliefs, and values and '. . . characterizes the experience of being between cultures' (Alfred, Byram and Fleming, 2003, p. 2). Playtexts that express different cultural perspectives and experiences allow students to engage with the personal stories of others in an intercultural way. The outcome of these experiences can develop cultural sensitivity and bring into sharp focus the cultural and social attitudes and beliefs of the participants (Donelan, 2002; Marshall, 2006). The educational value of intercultural learning is in its potential to provide students with opportunities to learn not only about others but also about themselves, encouraging students to develop a sense of relativity about his or her place in the world as they consider their own cultural values, beliefs and actions (Gupta, 2003, pp. 161–162). Matthew describes the outcomes of this research:

As a result of teaching the Indigenous play *The 7 Stage of Grieving* (Enoch et al., 1996), there was a change in knowledge, beliefs and values in my students. Using Giroux's theories of a post-colonial 'border pedagogy', we successfully constructed a politics that embraced difference and challenged injustice by focusing on representations and the way they produce meanings (Giroux, 1992, p. 29). The participants resisted a dialogue of closure by speaking with rather than for others. They grappled with their own cultural identity and engaged with 'a politics of location' by remapping the parameters of place, identity, history and power to understand how knowledge and power can be decentred (Giroux, 1992, p. 26). The activities related to the study of *The 7 Stages of Grieving* also led to a heightened cultural sensitivity. This outcome reflects Donelan's work (2005, p. 273) who found that dialogical relationships in intercultural performance projects encourage cultural respect. The students in this case study who chose to present group devised work mixed with scenes from *The 7 Stages of Grieving* navigated the rehearsal process and created a hybrid theatrical statement that gave voice to the Indigenous perspective in a culturally sensitive manner while challenging the dominant discourse through self-devised scenes. Two of the participants worked on a practical task together and when asked why they chose *The 7 Stages of Grieving* for their practical assessment, they highlighted their desire to create a performance where they addressed the ongoing incidents of oppression and racism and allowed the Indigenous Australian voice to be heard. This choice was especially interesting as early on in the unit, one of the participants' was cautious about working with *The 7 Stages of Grieving*: '*I am nervous about the challenge of performing an extract from 7 Stages . . . as I don't know how easy it will be to show a true representation of Aboriginal life without being racist or misrepresenting the situation*' (Oct. 19, 2007). Later in the unit, she explained why her feelings about the topic had changed; '*I guess putting our play together as well we were trying to think about of how it was reflected in society and how it questioned society and questioning like why is it still such a problem. And then I realised of course . . . ummm . . . what was I saying? . . . Because of the effect it has had it is still present*' (Dec. 3, 2007).

The students' final performance combined extracts from the play and scenes they had written. The bulk of their performance showed representations of Indigenous Australians, conveyed through role and symbol. The Australian Aboriginal flag was transformed at different points in the performance, for example bundled and carried gently as though a baby or laid out as though a parent in funeral repose. Its physical connection to the performers and evolving representations of meaning worked in strong contrast to the static use of the Australian flag that was draped over the front of a wooden lectern.

Some scenes showed wider social attitudes and targeted political figures well known for their intolerant and racist attitudes. The performance also referenced media representations and facts about Indigenous health, education and living standards interspersed with extracts from the play in a clever juxtaposition of the impact of misrepresentation set against the sobering factual information. In a particular scene, one of the performers stood upstage as the didactic voice of the media while the other performer contrasted this with a very focused and convincing performance as the Indigenous Everywoman.

The success of the this performance task for these students was made possible through a foundation of prior learning experiences that encouraged an engagement with culturally unfamiliar experiences and perspectives that resonated with the participants in both intellectual and emotional ways. The richness of the learning activities created a space where students could reflect on their own cultural identity in light of the historical, social and political backdrop of White and Indigenous relations in Australia. Learning that incorporates the kinaesthetic expression of an intercultural playtext encourages transformational learning. By encouraging the dynamic between thinking and feeling, teachers can create changes in understanding, increased self-awareness, reflection, imagination, enthusiasm, intelligent caring and a commitment to the well being of self and others. A highly desirable outcome if we wish to contribute to the development of active and informed citizens who are able to relate to and communicate across cultures. Matthew Clausen's intercultural investigations in his classroom reflect Jonothan Neelands' summation of the power of drama classroom as a space for cultural understanding:

> They have struggled to find a common culture in the classroom, in the playground, in the local streets. And drama has been part of this struggling towards a culture which transcends historical hatred and the fear of the other. A common culture which stands against persecution and prejudice and segregation. This is drama as a process of healing and being together. In this school drama has provided a powerful integrative force for bringing unfamiliar knowledge into knowing engagement. But it has also been a process of ensemble making. A way of modelling how through collective artistry, negotiation, contracting of behaviour and skilful leading, the ensemble in the classroom might become a model of how to live in the world. (Neelands, 2009a, p. 4)

Principles for collaborative learning

I would like to suggest some general principles that can be applied to the drama classroom to support and sustain collaborative learning. They are not the first and last word on the matter. For those interested in investigating this area further, I recommend the work of Jonothan Neelands, Matthew Clausen and Peter O'Connor. These principles can however underpin a robust and exciting collaborative learning space that is as Neelands might put it a 'rehearsal for life'.

1. Develop and support collaborative behaviour

Collaborative behaviours require structuring and scaffolding: in essence they need to be taught. Children collaborate and co-operate in social groups from when they first communicate. The precursor of this collaboration is the dramatic play where young children take on roles in the early years of learning. O'Toole et al. (2009) argue there is a long and proud tradition of leading educators valuing play in the classroom and play by its very nature is a collaborative and negotiated process. As Kelly-Byrne describes it: 'Play is as much the activity of oscillating in and out of the negotiations, or the metacommunications, as it is the dramatic content that these negotiations allow. In other words, the framing and negotiation are part of the metalanguage of play and are inseparable from its initiation and continuation' (1989, p. 242).

The first step in the development of collaborative learning is creating the circumstances where play and playfulness are prominent features of classroom learning. In drama improvisation provides a fertile ground for play and playfulness. While allowing play to develop and take its own course is crucial, there comes a time when play becomes more structured but playfulness continues in the more structured devising or script based drama learning activities. The imaginative experimentation in drama learning is the wellspring of creativity and will support the ongoing dynamism of drama learning. The following strategies will assist with developing and supporting dramatic play in the drama classroom.

- Make play part of the drama classroom culture
- Teach explicitly how collaboration that engages creativity operates by showing how ideas and approaches can be negotiated and created on a stage
- Explicitly teach negotiation behaviours; for example, how to make an offer and how to accept an offer
- Actively model collaborative behaviours in the classroom

2. Collaboration is not teacher absence

Some teachers have mistaken student collaboration as an excuse or opportunity for teacher absence. In my experience, the teacher's role in collaboration is pivotal. In the first instance, students need to understand the boundaries and the rules of engagement when it comes to collaboration. While the classroom should be a place for experimentation, the teacher's primary responsibility is to ensure the safety in all senses of students in their care. The first role is then to structure learning to allow collaboration to occur. When an effective collaborative classroom has been created, the next role of the teacher is to get involved in the collaborative drama making processes. Even skilled actors require the input and guidance of a skilled director. When young people have carriage of their own dramatic work, teachers will still need to provide their dramatic expertise to ensure that an idea becomes dramatically engaging. The extent to which this is required is always going to be a judgement call on behalf of the teacher. Too much direction and you risk stifling the creativity of your students. Too little and you risk your students' work not progressing beyond play and being dramatically unsatisfying.

Rather than being absent, the teacher should be in the middle of the learning as a co-creator and supporter of the making process. This role must be dealt with carefully. The responsibility of co-creation entails an understanding on behalf of the teacher of how to make students self-confident and self-sufficient in the making process. There is also a responsibility on teachers to allow students to express their own vision in the drama rather than the recycled vision of their teachers. The following strategies can assist teachers to make a constructive contribution to learning in drama:

- Demonstrate collaboration in your teacher-student relationships by negotiating the curriculum where possible
- Work with process drama techniques such as mantle of the expert and teacher in role to develop dramatic ideas and structures
- Work towards self-sustaining learning by intervening and assisting students to structure their drama
- Use side-coaching techniques during improvisation work to structure the performers and the audience's engagement with the work.

3. Create collaborative audiences

There is another role that deserves some attention and that is the collaboration of an attuned and engaged audience of peers. An attentive and constructively responsive audience does not just 'happen' it also needs to be taught. In that respect teachers also need to provide structures for audience response. Beyond the often knee-jerk 'I liked that' or 'I hated that', drama students should develop an analytical approach to their own work and the work of others whether that is in the theatre or in their own classrooms. Instead of expressing their views about their own preferences students should be encouraged by their teachers to express a view about what 'is working' and what 'is not working' dramatically in performances. While sometimes this will relate to the subject matter of the work it will in many cases refer more directly to the way the aesthetic is being controlled. The elements of drama provide an effective way of engaging with an analytical discussion around aesthetic control.

Building a culture of collaboration in audiences takes active structuring and engagement. Making audiences analytically responsive is a further challenge, but one worth attempting to create a classroom where collaboration is a prominent feature of the learning. You can build a collaborative audience by:

- Making your expectations of audience-actor interactions clear
- Teaching the analytical tools of drama such as the elements of drama
- Building a 'what if' approach to drama where students suggest other approaches
- Using analytical frameworks such as the elements of drama to encourage structured and thoughtful responses
- Encouraging student analytical feedback that engages clearly with dramatic form
- Encouraging students to draw on their own experience of drama practice to respond analytically. Such as using their understanding of Brechtian techniques or their experience of a recent professional performance to suggest ways to enhance the drama.

4. Assess collaboration effectively

One of the most pervasive catch cries in education is 'what matters gets assessed'. While I will deal with assessment in drama education in more detail in a later chapter it is worth making the point here that collaboration in the drama classroom can and should be assessed as a skill to be learnt, understood and demonstrated. If we agree with this principle we should search for ways to assess authentically the skills and approaches required for collaboration in learning generally such as negotiation, leadership, analysis and in drama specifically ensemble engagement, aesthetic control and the use of the dramatic and theatrical elements to create drama. We should avoid the tendency to overlay traditional testing regimes on dramatic learning processes that do not fit. This kind of approach produces inappropriate assessments that do not support learners or measure learning in any meaningful way. What I have in mind here is an essay on devising drama. A more effective assessment would examine collaboration as those processes are taking place and not rely on a downstream assessment that removes the assessment from the learning.

- Plan assessment when designing collaborative learning
- Use your assessment of collaborative learning to evaluate the effectiveness of your teaching as well as each students' individual learning
- Create effective criteria to ensure that students understand the standards that are expected from ensemble learning
- Design assessments which evaluate each student's individual contribution to the collaboration rather than relying only on a 'group mark'
- Build up work samples of effective collaboration to demonstrate what best practice collaboration in the drama classroom looks like.

5. Creating communities of practice

Communities of practice are present in many areas of our lives, especially in the world of work and schooling. The approach, based on the work of Vygotsky (1978), recognizes a shift from an individualistic cognitive approach to a sociocultural approach in education (Barab et al., 2002, p. 489) and theories of learning more generally (Walker, 2003, p. 226). Wenger (1998) defines a community of practice as a result of collective learning that: '. . . reflects both the pursuit of our enterprises and the attendant social relations. These practices are thus the property of a kind of community created over time by the sustained pursuit of a shared enterprise. It makes sense; therefore to call these kinds of communities, communities of practice' (1998, p. 45).

This last principle sums up what is possible when a group of learners and a teacher reach a level of effectiveness that transcends normative expectations of education. A community of practice is a group that has a shared understanding and set of skills that is applied to the task on hand. In the drama classroom, the community of practice is possible when learners have sufficient understanding of the art form to create drama that engages or even transports an audience. While I agree this is aspirational in many drama classes, it is nonetheless a goal worth pursuing so that the collaboration between teacher and student might achieve the dream that Neelands imagines (2009, p. 175) where the drama classroom is a model for civic harmony and collaboration.

Conclusions

Scottish-American industrialist and entrepreneur Andrew Carnegie said:

> Teamwork is the ability to work together toward a common vision; the ability to direct individual accomplishment toward organizational objectives. It is the fuel that allows common people to attain uncommon results.

I conclude with a quote from a businessman because I wanted to underscore the necessity of ensemble learning for young people – all young people. While it is true that some of our young people will use these skills on the stage and go onto theatrical careers, most will not. All of our students will need, however, to continue learning from others who differ from themselves and almost all of them will need to understand how to work in teams. This interpersonal understanding is an essential part of our modern democratic world, and it is one of the reasons drama has historically, and still today, has a strong case for being part of the mandatory curriculum. If our communities and their governments are serious about creating democratic, pluralistic societies that not only tolerate but understand and engage with difference, drama would be at the centre of the curriculum. Drama teachers have a responsibility to make the case for the value of ensemble learning and to make plain how drama is one of the few sites in the curriculum that actively teaches and encourages collaborative understanding in ensemble learning.

In Part II, I would like to build on the foundations discussed in Chapters One to Five to explore some of the practical issues in drama teaching. The next chapter, 'Planning Drama Learning', examines some of the features of planning effective drama education experiences for students.

Part II
Teaching Drama with Generation Next: Pedagogy in Practice

Planning Drama Learning **6**

Killing *The Merchant of Venice*

One of my strongest memories from high school English was the way I learnt about Shakespeare. It is probably a scene familiar to anyone who was educated in the last 30 years. The scene is a cold classroom on a Wednesday afternoon just before we were all released to play sport. The feeling of pent up energy in the room was palpable in the all male class (including the teacher). We were being introduced to the 'wonders of Shakespeare' through the traditional reading-around-the-class method. You are probably familiar with this hackneyed approach. One student reads a part without preparation, and then another student takes a part. At its best, this provides a static and uninspired 'coverage of the content of the text'; at worst, it confirms the suspicions of most students that Shakespeare's language is inaccessible and his drama too hard to understand. In my case, *The Merchant of Venice* was being systematically drained of all its drama by a teacher who perhaps had respect for Shakespeare's great play, but not much idea how to awaken the drama in this great work. It often strikes me that with a little more preparation by that well meaning teacher, the depths of that play could have been uncovered for me, that the meaning of the '*The quality of mercy is not strained. It droppeth as the gentle rain from heaven. Upon the place beneath. It is twice blest: It blesseth him that gives and him that takes' (Act IV, Scene I)* could have been powerfully realized.

I can only marvel at Shakespeare's brilliance that many students who have endured this kind of approach come out the other side still appreciating Shakespeare. Flash forward about 20 years. A skilled teacher/actor from a major Shakespeare company is working with a room full of teachers, talking about planning to teach the drama of Shakespeare. The teacher/actor asks the question, 'how do we get your students to understand how thrilling this play is'. Various suggestions come forward, but all had one thing in common; all these teachers, many of them English teachers, understood that plays are about more than the content. Their suggestions included watching performances or excerpts of performances, improvisations around the content of the play and making various scenes of the play for performance. These teachers recognized that plays are about live interactions. If this vignette is contextualized in terms of aesthetic control and aesthetic understanding, these teachers have made the crucial link between students understanding the aesthetics of drama (watching performances or excerpts of performances) and controlling the aesthetics of Shakespearean drama (making various moments of the play for performance).

Although this may not look like planning, it is. These teachers are demonstrating highly effective planning strategies because they are planning for engagement. In my experience, engagement is one of the most crucial factors in effective learning. This may be a surprising position to take in a world of objectives, aims, outcomes and schemes of work, but if there is no engagement none of these structures are relevant. The first principle of effective planning in drama and probably all learning is about engaging students in what they are about to learn.

I am going to approach planning as a process rather than a product. Planning for drama learning in my view is more involved than ticking off outcomes, objectives or developing schemes of work. I would like to concentrate on what might make drama learning engaging and enticing for students and at the same time create deep learning for young people in drama education.

Planning learning in drama has some unique elements, and what I will explore here is how drama teachers can integrate practical, experiential and aesthetic learning in their planning processes. I will discuss outcome-based learning, objectives, aims and schemes of work and conclude with a discussion of the principles for effective planning for drama learning.

About engagement

Recent research (Munns et al., 2006) into engagement among young people identifies two levels of engagement: 'e'ngagement, which refers to young people being in-task in affective, cognitive and operative ways, and 'E'ngagement, which refers to a more enduring engagement with learning processes and structures where young people become 'insiders' within a community of practice (Durrant and Green, 2000). Researchers argue that for students to become 'E'ngaged in learning environments, they need powerful messages around concepts of knowledge, ability, control, place and voice (Munns et al., 2006). Research into drama programs with young people suggests that when participants are e/Engaged in drama programs (such as playwriting), they become more confident, creative, and aware of social justice issues (Dupré, 2006; Woolland, 2008; Chizhik, 2009). Given that engagement is crucial, let us explore how engagement can be made central to the process of planning drama learning.

Maps and mapmaking: planning drama

Research into teacher planning reflects what we could probably already have guessed, teachers spend a large part of their time planning (Groundwater-Smith et al., 2007). Planning is not only the artefact, the piece of paper. The scheme of work or program or learning activity is really only a map. Perhaps most of the time spent planning is in the brain, not on paper, where all of the experience, understanding and specific contextual factors of the planning process occur. In this sense, teachers are mapmakers, surveying the landscape and using their experience and understanding of the contours to create a map for themselves and others to follow.

The exact recipe for planning in any subject is not always clear because '. . . teachers must balance the curriculum decisions made by other people and groups – syllabus, policy makers and mandated perspectives – with their own belief systems' (Groundwater-Smith et al., 2007, p. 187). Planning about learning according to Susan Groundwater-Smith relates to a series of external and internal factors that relate to specific teachers in their unique contexts including:

External factors

The community of the school
Parental expectations
Social diversity and background of the students
Funding and resources
Syllabus, curriculum and school policies

Internal Factors

Perceived decision making space (Smith and Lovat, 2003)
Teacher beliefs about how students learn most effectively
Perceptions about student expectations of the discipline
Teacher's own beliefs about their ability to teach effectively

Planning for the twenty-first century

Earlier in this book, I discussed how resistant schools and schooling have been to change. One way to combat and respond effectively is to prioritize in your planning to respond to the realities of the twenty-first century rather than the nineteenth century. I would like to nominate some 'planning themes' that should contribute to a contemporary approach to planning, if not a future orientation. By this, I mean if your programs build on these themes, they can be directly relevant to the needs, interests and aspirations of your students now and contribute to their development as citizens in the community that they will make for themselves and others.

Features of planning for drama learning

When drama teachers are planning learning, there are more than a few specific features of drama that will differentiate this process from planning in other subject areas such as mathematics, history or English. Jonothan Neelands outlined more than a decade ago the similarities between drama pedagogy and a well crafted theatrical production: he advises: 'The sequencing of the lesson needs to be as subtle and as crafted as any other dramatic sequence that is planned to unfold its meanings or theme in time and space and which moves the audience, progressively, towards a new-felt understanding of the human issues that are being dramatised' (Neelands, 1998, p. 58).

Discussions of planning in mainstream preservice teacher textbooks often begin with advice about meeting objectives such as 'Learning in a school environment is frequently goal-directed. Students are at school because they want to learn certain things, attain specific standards . . .' (Marsh, 2004, p. 123). While there may be truth in this for many teachers and students in several subjects, the reality for teachers in the arts dealing with creative processes is more complex. As David Wright (2005) explains, the mind and body are fully engaged in drama:

> The structure of learning in drama is such that the emergent cannot be anticipated or known in full beforehand. Furthermore, it cannot be generated simply because it is (or is assumed to be) known . . . . It is a consequence of the recursive processes of reflection and improvisation. These processes can generate challenging and unpredictable results. Drama teachers work with this sort of 'unfolding logic' day in and day out. It is here that teachers, as much as students, must consider themselves 'participants in' something they can only partly know (and/or determine). This is at odds with conventional pedagogic practice. (2005, p. 2)

The nature of the 'unfolding logic' of creativity is a process of trial and error, and in many cases does not present a product or an artefact that is easily measured against an outcome, an objective or an aim. Take for instance a drama teacher planning a lesson of work to explore playbuilding. To teach this skill, students often work in groups with a stimulus that develops through improvisation into text and then sometimes but not necessarily into a full performance. There are several process related learning activities that do not always fit neatly within outcomes, aims or objectives such as how to understand and respond to theatrical ideas in playbuilding. While in a summative sense that could be demonstrated at the end of a playbuilding process, it is not easily measured in process in an authentic way. So as drama teachers, we should be aware that much of the learning that is central to our area does not always conform to an outcome, aim or objective.

Outcomes-based education and drama

The outcomes-based approach pioneered by Bill Spady represented a shift from input model that is classically characterized as the tipping of teacher generated knowledge into student's minds like the filling of empty vessels. The outcomes approach was an attempt to conceptualize learning by showing what students can do. Leading arts educator, Robyn Ewing describes the philosophy behind the Spady's approach. She argues it is '. . . the realisation of the objectives model but in reality it begins from a different orientation to curriculum and learning. It originated from a desire to have all learners experience success and emerge as capable learners . . .' (Ewing, 2010, p. 31). The criticisms of outcomes-based education have emerged as teachers sometimes struggle to implement a bureaucratic version of the original concept in diverse curriculum, school and subject contexts (Ewing, 2010, p. 36). In my experience, drama teachers sometimes find the outcomes-based approach a slightly odd fit with the demands of creativity learning specifically, and drama learning in particular. Planning for creativity learning has some important implications for the way we construct learning. I will outline some of the themes in no particular order and provide some suggestions about how we might work to incorporate them in drama planning.

Planning for embodied learning

Mostly the body is ignored in education. Apart perhaps from physical education, dance and drama, Ken Robinson's famous description of schooling's approach to the body rings true: 'They look upon their body as a form of transport for their heads, don't they?' (Robinson, 2001). We have discussed the unique place of embodiment in the drama classroom earlier, but it does bear reinforcing when we turn our mind to how it might be planned for in drama learning. Lynn Fels (2009) describes the complexity of embodied learning and the research of this process (bolding in original): '**Embodied** within my own understanding of complexity in education and performative inquiry is the interplay of breath, presence, and absence within the intimacy of relationship, time, engagement, inquiry, language, and location' (Fels, 2009, p. 140).

Her analysis of the processes of embodied learning identifies the explicit and tacit features of drama learning. In my view, there is so much learning going on that teachers can miss crucial opportunities if they choose not to integrate all of these ideas into our planning. Let us consider a scheme of work that is exploring Tracy Letts' darkly comic American tale of a family in continual decline, *August: Osage County*. Planning a drama learning experience here that engages and inspires students demands that the characters be embodied so the complexity that Lynn Fels identifies (2009, p. 142) in 'the intimacy of relationship, time, engagement, inquiry, language, and location' is communicated at first to students in the learning process and ultimately in the performance of the play. To achieve aesthetic understanding of any play, and especially one that is as character-driven as *August: Osage County*, reading or even watching the play will not give the depth of understanding required for the characterization and dramatic action of the play. To achieve that level of understanding, the characters and the action of the play need to be embodied by the learner. Planning in this way brings its own complexities even in an age when we understand knowing as more than a cerebral phenomenon. If the benefits of drama education are to be made available to increased numbers of students, there is a need for those who want this to happen to reflect more upon the systemic dynamics of embodied learning and make it happen in their classroom.

Planning for creativity

One of the persistent myths about creativity and learning is that it cannot be taught or planned for. This view suggests that creativity is inborn and cannot be learned, enhanced and developed in any way. The research evidence suggests that creativity can be developed, taught and supported in schools and other places (Sternberg, 2006). Sometimes creative thinking challenges schools and other systems. Effective teaching and creative teaching is one and the same thing. If you are to teach your student's creativity in the context of drama, you must approach your own pedagogy with a creative orientation. Teaching in this way will see the teacher work flexibly, drawing from all their pedagogical skills. As *All Our Futures* suggests, there is '. . . a balance in all good teaching between formal instruction of content and of skills, and giving young people the freedom to inquire, question, experiment and to express their own thoughts and ideas' (NACCE, 1999, p. 105). If you as the teacher are able to teach creatively, then the preconditions are emerging to teach creativity. Teaching creativity is an awkward idea because the pedagogy demands flexibility and innovation that is in direct conflict with the proscription and testing-based curriculum that is so prevalent in many Western education systems (Abbs, 2003, p. 1). Effective teaching for creativity will model creativity and provide learning experiences that support its growth in students. The National Advisory Committee on Creative and Cultural Education (NACCE) sums up the tensions that arise from the idea of 'teaching' creativity: They argue: 'There is an obvious sense in which children cannot be "taught" creativity in the way that they can be taught the times tables. Creative processes do draw from knowledge and practical skills. It is also the case that there are various techniques to facilitate creative thinking' (NACCE, 1999, p. 103).

The development of creativity in drama and to a large extent all the arts sees the melding of aesthetic control and aesthetic understanding. In this process, there will be times when students are left to experiment and others when students are taught more directly the principles of the art form that they are working within. The modelling of creative approaches has the potential to deliver rich learning experiences that foster innovation and creativity rather than teach students to produce facile and derivative work. Before we proceed with further discussions about creativity, it may be worth identifying and discussing some of the persistent myths about creativity learning that may hinder our approach to teaching, and in particular developing sustainable planning for creativity learning in drama education.

Creativity is for the gifted, chosen few

One of the dominant myths that surrounds creativity is that it is only available to the elite gifted few. You often hear in industries such as theatre, film and advertising the term 'creatives' used. This nomenclature is designed to delineate the 'creatives' from the 'non-creatives' or the more widely used euphemism, the technicians. This dichotomy entrenches the old idea that some are born to creativity and some are born to technicality as if these two cannot interact. Of course, the technicians often practice a great deal of creativity. In the making of theatre if those who are called 'creatives' have no understanding of the technical aspects of their work, their creativity is likely to founder. Aesthetic control and understanding is always predicated on a sound base of technical understanding.

Creativity is part of our daily lives and exercised by us all. Craft (2002) calls this 'lifewide creativity' because it is present and demonstrated everyday and seen not just in education. This is the starting point for drama learning. Drama learning is an educative process that begins with the students' immersion in dramatic making and appreciating processes, and then seeks to build aesthetic understanding and aesthetic control in the art form. For instance, when students first begin to understand and develop characters, they have begun a creative process. While this may be seen by some as elementary in the development of student's understanding of drama, it is original for the individual student. The Robinson report (1999) nominates originality as a feature of creativity. Most importantly, it defines originality as original for the individual involved in the activity. This is a fundamentally democratic approach to creativity (Robinson, 1999) that frees educators to focus their pedagogy on all students rather than just those that might one day have the potential genius required for a more restricted definition of creativity. This approach does not deny that there are different qualities of creativity; it simply argues that all students, provided with the necessary resources, can be creative.

Creativity is individual and not collaborative

In some places, creativity has been depicted as an individual's struggle for greatness devoid of any real support. Just them, often starving in a garret writing the next great novel, play, film and so on. This is perhaps the most debilitating and anti-intuitive myth that relates to creativity for arts educators – that it is an individualistic cognitive skill that has no relationship to others. As Fischer et al. (2005) argues: 'Much human creativity arises from activities that take place in a social context in which interactions with other people and the artefacts that embody group knowledge are important contributors to the process. Creativity does not happen inside a person's head, but in the interaction between a person's thoughts and a socio-cultural context' (2005, p. 485). This complexity may be difficult to measure with tests, but it is a truism of creativity in arts learning that it is not an isolated cognitive skill, but rather a complex interaction of the individual learner, their learning context, their fellow learners and the aesthetic.

A cursory understanding of the collaborative processes involved in drama, music and film argues against this stereotype of creativity. For drama in particular, it is very much the exception that the individual is capable of creating theatre. Creativity in these areas routinely relies on the interplay of several creative approaches at once for anything to be created. While research has focussed more heavily on the sources of individual and personal creativity (Jeffrey and Craft, 2001), there is evidence that creativity can and is achieved in group contexts. Mahn and John-Steiner (2002) argue that in collaboration, participants create mutual zones of proximal development[1] for each other where their intellect and emotions are brought together in a unified whole. They explain how they think collaborative creativity actually works: 'In producing texts, partners share each other's early drafts; they strive to give shape to their communicative intent by combining precision – or word meaning- with the fluidity of the sense of the words. They live, temporarily, in each other's heads. They also draw on their mutuality as well as their differences in knowledge, working styles and temperament' (2002, p. 51).

The same processes are taking place in drama learning. For instance if students are involved in a playbuilding process they may develop an idea from a stimulus that is then developed further through improvisation and then worked into a performance perhaps through a theatrical style or form they have learnt about, perhaps in this case a Brechtian performance style they learnt through studying *Mother Courage*. So you might expect in this improvisation the use of the distancing effect (Erikkson, 2009) and the use of direct address to an audience and harsh stage lighting. The learning taking place here relies on the student to work with the group in cooperating with the understanding they have of the aesthetic demands of the form.

As teachers who have worked in the arts know well, the products of these collaborations are not always high quality. They are often banal and plodding, but the potential for creativity is enhanced when the teacher is able to develop a learning environment that makes aesthetic control and aesthetic understanding prominent. Learning to be creative is an evolutionary growth that begins with the student making original discoveries (for themselves) and then building on those discoveries in a broader social context. If we accept that we as drama teachers are actually in the business of creativity learning, it will allow us to respond to the drive for outcomes, aims and objectives forcefully. Our argument should always be that creativity learning has never and will never be about an individual pursuit for the chosen few gifted students, but it will rather be a learning process that has much trial and error, much collaboration and frequent dead ends that do not always produce a finished work. If we are convinced of this and we can convince our colleagues of this, outcomes-based education does not need to be a rod for the drama teacher's back.

Planning for multiliteracies

Teachers have absorbed literacy in their planning processes for a long time now. They do this in most cases because they understand that literacy is directly linked to social mobility and the health of our democracy (hooks, 2003). The work of the New London Group that began in 1994 has allowed the traditional understanding of literacy as a language-bound pedagogy to be transformed into a discussion of multiple literacies or multiliteracies to take account of the diversity of cultures and media that make up modern communication. The implications for drama teachers are that learners arrive in their classrooms with diverse cultural understandings that are derived from diverse backgrounds. In addition, students have expectations and understandings born of their experience with the digitally networked society. Drama teachers are well placed to engage with this classroom reality if they plan effectively for it and not just recognize it exists, but actively work with multiliteracies to develop dynamic classrooms.

In the discussion of literacy, there are terms that have the potential to be confusing. In this discussion, when I refer to 'literacy', I mean the traditional forms of literacy. The *Oxford English Dictionary* (2006) defines this as 'The quality or state of being literate; knowledge of letters; condition in respect to education, esp. ability to read and write'. Multiliteracy is defined here as literacy that embraces digital and other texts. Let's begin with a discussion of the place of literacy in today's classrooms.

Linking creativity and literacy allows young people to design their own future and engage with issues that relate to their worlds. It recognizes that they have a responsibility to interpret current social construction, but also to create the new worlds that they and their descendants will inhabit. In the New London Groups (NLG, 1996) introduction of multiliteracy theory, the crucial and under-recognized link is made by the NLG between creativity and literacy. They argue that people design meaning through a process that recognizes 'available designs' and creates new ones. They argue, 'In an economy of productive diversity, in civic spaces that value pluralism, and in the flourishing of interrelated, multilayered, complementary yet increasingly divergent lifeworlds, workers, citizens, and community members are ideally creative and responsible makers of meaning. We are, indeed, designers of our social futures' (NLG, 1996, p. 88).

The narrow political posturing that sometimes passes for debate in this area often reduces the debate about literacy to a cliché. This is irritating and concerning because there are significant issues of social justice and access to cultural capital that narrow political positions tend to overshadow. As bell hooks argues: 'When teachers support democratic education we automatically support widespread literacy . . . . Everyone that knows how to read and write has the tools to enter higher learning even if that learning cannot and does not take place in a university setting' (hooks, 2003, p. 43).

Literacy has a vital role to play in providing all students with the opportunity to democratically engage with their community. The critical literacies approach commits this kind of aspiration to action. The approach is heavily influenced by the work of Paulo Friere who stressed the importance of active learning rather than traditional direct instructional models of filling 'empty vessels'. Luke and Freebody argue that those practising critical literacies are '. . . a coalition of educational interests committed to engaging with the possibilities that technologies of writing and other modes of inscription offer for social change, cultural diversity, economic equity and, political enfranchisement' (1997, p. 1). This social change potentially comes about when citizens focus on and question the context and the motivation of the messages they are bombarded with.

While critical literacy may seem like the very basis of education, for many educators it has garnered significant criticism from 'traditionalists'. Kenneth Wiltshire wrote:

> By its own admission it [critical literacy] is about things such as revealing the purpose and motives of the composers of texts and their lack of neutrality, the way alternative views are silenced, the power of language, providing students with opportunities to clarify their own attitudes and values, take a stance on issues and take social action . . . . This sort of thinking is a recipe for laziness, indifference and unwillingness to identify standards and common values. It inevitably leads to dumbing down of the curriculum and therefore the students . . . . Should *The Diary of Anne Frank* be replaced with *The Emails of Tom Cruise* or *The Text Messages of Shane Warne*? (*The Australian*, 23 September, 2006)

What this critique of critical literacy uncovers is two concerns. The first is whether messages should be analysed with reference to their context and the second is that any form of communication that is electronically mediated is less valid than the printed word. The effect of this kind of criticism diminishes the importance of understanding multiple messages and their sources. Its denigration of emerging literacies resorts to the lowest common denominator of celebrity trivia. While this has been a popular stalking horse of political conservatives, there is little evidence that any education system has seriously gone to the excesses depicted here. That educators would seriously consider teaching trivia rather than literature underestimates the professionalism of teachers generally.

Teachers of drama will need to defend critical literacy as a valid and indeed prominent way of examining their subject matter. Medina et al. (2007) argue that drama can

> . . . provide spaces where intense personal reflection is mediated through complex social interactions within the creation of fictional worlds. When positioned critically, these interactions necessitate the juxtaposition of participant ideologies. Once accessed for the facilitation of the character's needs, these ideologies are made apparent and scrutinized. It is through this scrutiny that positions of power and domination may be explored. (2007, p. 125).

The ability to analyse and then respond to theatre, be it William Shakespeare's *Macbeth*, Caryl Churchill's *Top Girls* or David Hare's *Gethsemane*, is central to the practice of making and appreciating classical and more contemporary drama. Arguments that focus on whether young people should examine Moliere (*The Misanthrope*) rather than David Mamet (*Speed the Plow*) or Polly Stenham (*That Face*) are distractions at best. Drama teachers should draw from the best of all traditions to support the learning of students and ignore the trivial and aesthetically bankrupt.

Unfortunately, the political posturing that sometimes surrounds the debates about literacy has the potential to pigeonhole this area of learning and restrict students' access to literacy that is relevant and relates directly to the world they inhabit. As the New London Group argue: 'Literacy pedagogy has traditionally meant teaching and learning to read and write in a page-bound, official, standard forms of the national language. Literacy pedagogy, in other words, has been a carefully restricted project – restricted to formalised, monolingual, monocultural and rule governed forms of language' (NLG, 1996, p. 61).

The proponents of multiliteracy argue that it is no longer sufficient to pretend that the printed word is the dominant media. In modern societies, diversity and the prevalence of digital technologies requires a literacy that will support readings and creation in multiple forms of literacy. The implications for developing critical, active and democratic citizens from our schools are that our students will need to interpret and create messages beyond the written word. If they are to do this effectively, schooling must engage with literacy forms beyond the printed page. While this theory has come to currency lately, multiliteracy as a social practice has been around perhaps before the written word. Elizabeth Daley argues that multiliteracy was the first literacy. She says: 'The concept of a language composed of elements other than word and text is neither fundamentally new or particularly revolutionary. Rather, this concept is an evolutionary development of the ideas and practices that have been with us since people first struggled to leave records and tell stories' (Daley, 2003, p. 187).

To investigate the implications for teacher planning, let us look at how a teacher might plan the development of a scripted piece of drama. Let us take the text that we started with, Shakespeare's *Merchant of Venice*. A critical literacy approach to this text would recognize that there are some fairly contested cultural representations of ethnicity and religion on display that bear examination and debate. Students might be encouraged to discuss the motivation of the characters from their own perspective but more importantly for the drama classroom, how these characters might be directed to create dramatic meaning for an audience. Going back to our earlier discussion, this will involve trial and error, working with the characters in space, but it will allow students to engage with how character attitudes become real for an audience and perhaps more importantly allows them to take differing perspectives on a given problem. Another component of multiliteracies asks us to consider how messages might be created beyond the written and spoken word. Often this aspect of multiliteracies is assumed to be the way technology creates alternate ways of communicating, but the theatre has been communicating in non-verbal ways for thousands of years. Consider the ways the mise en scene of the set creates meaning, or the way music creates mood or the way gesture can reinforce or undermine the meaning of dialogue. There are rich pickings here for teachers interested in going beyond the verbal and perhaps a case for theatre being one of the richest and most complex settings to explore multiliteracies in action.

Planning for empathic decision-making and action

One of the persistent claims of drama education is that students develop intrapersonal (self) and interpersonal (between people) understanding. For our purposes, I would like to simplify this a little and refer to drama's ability to create empathy and go further to create imagined and potentially real life action.

As teachers of drama, the work of examining character and creating collaborative dramatic work is a site of emotional learning. As Arnold and Hughes (2005) argue: 'The nature of drama in education lends itself to the realisation of enthusiasm, empathy, engagement and confident expression of expertise'. This does not happen by accident and experienced teachers can see the change in students as they grow in this personal knowledge. While more research is required to create a firm evidence base for this claim, on the basis of the evidence available, drama learning provides a space for interpersonal learning to occur. One example of the way drama educators plan for this can be seen in the work of leading drama educator Peter O'Connor's Everyday Theatre. Everyday Theatre is a government-department funded applied theatre program focusing on family violence, child abuse and neglect that has worked with over 15,000 children aged 10–12 years across New Zealand. The focus of this work is to create emotional understanding among young people. Chris Holland (2009) evaluated this program and made the following observations about how empathic learning is created:

> The skill, understanding, respect and empathy for students is always present in teachers themselves, as they work through the conventions. Their skilfully dramatic depictions of characters move students deeper into the drama. Where appropriate, the teacher/actors challenge the students to reflect and refine their thinking, enabling them to 'know better what they already know'. Their supportive, highly skilled and sensitive questioning protects students into empathic decision-making and action. The teacher/actors show confidence in and respect towards the students, by never forcing them, but instead constantly adjusting the programme and providing safe ways for students to express themselves and learn. (2009, p. 542)

The planning process here is embodied within the teaching practice, according to Holland. While it might be difficult to show this kind of planning in a scheme of work, a program or a series of aims or outcomes, the preparation is still evident in practice, 'highly skilled and sensitive questioning that protects students into empathic decision-making and action'. This teaching skill needs to be planned and is evident in the work of drama practitioners such as Andy Kempe, Jonothan Neelands, Helen Nicholson and Dorothy Heathcote who through sometimes very different approaches exhibit a sensitivity and an understanding to the potential for theatre to create empathic understanding. If our students do gain a deeper understanding of how to understand themselves and others, it will perhaps support the next theme, planning for democracy.

Planning for democratic understanding

As a way to reiterate that argument for democratic education, it might be worth a reminder of what democratic schooling is, why it is important and what it might look like in the classroom.

Drawing on the work of Karl Popper, Cohen and Manion (2004) argue that (italics in original): '*Respect* for difference rather than merely tolerance of it, is central, as we learn from difference and dissent. Teachers, Popper suggests, have the task of educating developing minds to think critically and democratically, so that open society can flourish. Democracy *requires* education, and free speech in a democracy must require its free speakers to have something to say' (2004, p. 9). Again planning for democracy cannot necessarily be found in the artefacts of planning (schemes of work), although it might be. It is the development of a climate of learning that values diversity that prizes respectful dissent and nurtures debate. All of this sounds a little utopian when considered in the context of Year 9 on a rainy Wednesday afternoon. But perhaps before we move to how it might work in practice it might be useful to clarify what it is not.

In my view, democratic classrooms do not always allow students to dictate or even choose their learning. This is difficult at best in most schooling systems. What I am suggesting rather is that we enliven our classrooms by allowing our students to use their explorations in drama to test their ideas and the ideas of others. To achieve this, we have our art form as the starting point. There are any number of plays that challenge societal norms and ask difficult questions of society. The works of Howard Barker, David Mamet, Ariel Dorfman, David Hare, Joanna Murray-Smith, Tom Stoppard and Caryl Churchill all engage their characters in situations that provide stimulus for decisions around democracy, diversity and human rights. Take for example the following classic speech by Nora and Torvald Helmer from Henrik Ibsen's *A Doll's House*:

Helmer:	I would gladly work night and day for you, Nora – bear sorrow and want for your sake. But no man would sacrifice his honour for the one he loves.
Nora:	It is a thing hundreds of thousands of women have done.
Helmer:	Oh, you think and talk like a heedless child.
Nora:	Maybe. But you neither think nor talk like the man I could bind myself to. As soon as your fear was over, and it was not fear for what threatened me, but for what might happen to you when the whole thing was past, as far as you were concerned it was exactly as if nothing at all had happened. Exactly as before, I was your little skylark, your doll, which you would in future treat with doubly gentle care, because it was so brittle and fragile. (Getting up.) Torvald it was then it dawned upon me that for eight years I had been living here with a strange man, and had borne him three children. Oh, I can't bear to think of it! I could tear myself into little bits!
Helmer:	(sadly) I see, I see. An abyss has opened between us there is no denying it. But, Nora, would it not be possible to fill it up?
Nora:	As I am now, I am no wife for you.
Helmer:	I have it in me to become a different man.
Nora:	Perhaps if your doll is taken away from you.
Helmer:	But to part! to part from you! No, no, Nora, I can't understand that idea.
Nora:	(going out to the right) That makes it all the more certain that it must be done. (She comes back with her cloak and hat and a small bag which she puts on a chair by the table.)
Helmer:	Nora, Nora, not now! Wait until tomorrow.
Nora:	(putting on her cloak) I cannot spend the night in a strange man's room.

This is a well known text that is a rich stimulus for a critical, engaged and dynamic discussion. Working with this text provides a diversity of views on gender roles, power and the rights of the person. Activities that deal with Nora's motivations and choices, Torvald's motivations and choices and how all of these relate to the choices we face today are fertile ground for classroom exploration. You may have noted that the teachers still have an active presence in this process. They are leading the learning by choosing a promising pretext and letting the skill of the dramatist raise questions of democracy, diversity and choice. This activity is not a handover of responsibility for learning. The drama teacher has always and will always have that responsibility. It is also not in this case a process of negotiated curriculum. Sadly, that has become less and less possible as educational governing bodies have become more restrictive. To the extent that this is possible and feasible, negotiating curriculum should still be attempted. This example is designed to engage students as they ask questions of themselves and of their society, about what is ethical, about what is normal and about what is the democratic right of each member of that society. In the final analysis of our worth in the lives of young people, it may not be the things we have taught them about, for instance, acting or design that matter. In my view, it will be those things we have taught them about living critically, democratically and ethically in a diverse society that will really be the mark of our effectiveness as drama educators. Or as Jonothan Neelands puts it:

> The social experience of acting as an ensemble, making theatre that reflects and suggests how the world might become, in the hope that it is not finished, is of course of paramount importance to our young. We pass them the burden of the world that we have made in the hope that they will in turn have a world to pass on to their children. In this task socially made theatre will be their mirror, dynamo and lens-their tool for change. (2010, p. 156)

Some principles for effective planning in drama learning

So to summarize and conclude, let us revisit some of the key ideas in planning for drama learning.

Planning is about developing a map but knowing not all plans are on paper

As I hope I have made abundantly clear, planning is as much about understanding your students and your school context and bringing your understanding of drama to bear on that context. Of course there will always be a need to record what you are doing or where you are planning to go in a program or a scheme of work, but that document is only useful if it produces great learning. A document by itself is only worth the paper it is written on (literally) if the skills of the teacher cannot create vibrant and active learning. As teachers, we are not only map readers; we must be skilled mapmakers as well.

Plan for a living experience of drama

There is some research evidence that students who are involved in the arts are more engaged and motivated across the curriculum (Hetland and Winner, 2001; Anderson and Gibson, 2008). In my experience as a teacher, this certainly seems to be the case but more research is required to confirm the hunches arts teachers have about this. These hunches are currently the subject of large international research[2] so we may see some evidence that relates to this question very soon. In the meantime, what I know from my experience as a teacher is that the drama classroom can create a learning space that is different and potentially more appealing for some students. The drama classroom at its best is creative, experimental, physical and critical. All these features are contextualized within the aesthetics of drama and theatre. When this is all planned and works effectively, we see as Neelands (2004) calls it, 'living experience of drama'. It comes to fruition through well planned and engaging learning.

Effective drama plans encourage emergent learning

Learning in drama is a somewhat evolutionary process. Ideas emerge and then grow as we add layers of meaning to them. Consider the development of a student-devised performance. It begins perhaps with a stimulus or a pretext and then grows as layers of meaning are added such as design, direction and acting. In the end, we have a performance that has transformed often from a seed of an idea to become something with dimension, and ideally complexity and sophistication. Planning for this process is not straightforward. It requires teachers to think about the many and varied paths that the learning might take while still considering how the mandated system of systemic requirements can be met. It is made possible by structuring learning experiences that are inherently flexible but that pursue the core learning in drama: creating a character or role, devising dramatic work, making drama from literature and developing understanding of yourself and others.

Effective drama plans encourage divergent, connected and deep learning

As I mentioned in the opening chapters, drama has the potential to be *the* productive pedagogy (more on this in the next chapter). The aesthetic of the art form is a collector of other art forms including visual arts and design, music, literature and dance. It also has the added advantage of being an art form that questions societal assumptions and challenges the status quo. As a classroom drama teacher, nirvana classroom is one where all knowledge mixes and bounces on each other in the attempt to make great drama. While this is probably a rare occurrence when it does happen, you can almost see the synaptic connections students are making between ideas and approaches in the attempt to connect several, sometimes competing ideas and resolve those ideas into a performance. This kind of problem solving is demanding for students, but in planning drama learning we should be aspirational for our students. Rather than underestimating their abilities and the power of the art form, we should plan learning that inspires our students to connect knowledge with drama to create meaning for themselves and their audiences.

Effective drama learning uses the aesthetic to help students understand themselves, others and their society

I have reviewed many of the arguments between drama and theatre in the earlier chapters, but ultimately we need to ask ourselves the philosophical question as drama teachers. What will students learn and do as a result of our teaching? In my view, they will grow a deeper and better understanding of the power and dynamism of the theatre, but more crucially they will learn that theatre is a powerful way to learn about themselves and the world around them. In this sense, drama is social and personal learning that uses the power of the aesthetic as a way to explore human experience. In this way, drama learning is directly analogous to the theatre with the shift away from the audience experience to the participant experience being central in the drama classroom. When planning for social learning, we should be cognizant of the potential drama has for this kind of learning. As demonstrated in the extract from *A Doll's House,* well-planned drama learning is perhaps the most effective place to explore broader issues. When planning drama in your classroom, consider how the aesthetic understanding can lead to broader learning and how that can be created as a deliberate approach to your students understanding of the subject.

Conclusions

There are several challenges to face when planning drama learning. These challenges arise from two fundamentally different places. The first challenge arises from a schooling system that may demand outcomes for learning that is as much process driven as it is outcomes driven, and that is true whether you are creating a performance or developing a teacher in role learning activity. In the face of this challenge, drama educators must argue for the uniqueness of their learning area and demand that systems fit them rather than the system dictating structures that are fundamentally restrictive to student learning in the arts.

The second challenge arises from the sheer potential and complexity of learning in drama. Some of the planning principles I have alluded to here are downright difficult to plan for because they rely on a flexible, open approach that also demands of the teacher the skills of an instructor, guide, director, a facilitator (and more) and sometimes all these roles at once. Planning, like teaching drama, demands that we develop multiple personas that we employ to make drama learning effective. While this sounds ominous at the outset, it is possible if our mapmaking (our developing understanding of drama learning) and our maps (the artefacts of learning: the schemes of work and so on) are infused with flexibility and an understanding of the power of a classroom where embodied, social and creative learning is possible.

You will be familiar with what bad planning looks like, it can be seen in the eyes of bored disengaged students like the ones who endured *The Merchant of Venice* lesson on the rainy Wednesday afternoon. Good planning will not always lead to 'mountain top' learning experiences, but an approach that values and trusts the aesthetic is likely to create an environment where deep, connected and engaged learning is possible. Surely that is the most important aim we can have as teachers.

Notes

1 The Zone of Proximal Development (ZPD) is the term created by Lev Vygotsky to describe 'The distance between the actual developmental level as determined by independent problem solving and the level of potential development as determined through problem solving under adult guidance, or in collaboration with more capable peers' (Vygotsky, 1978, p. 86).

2 I am referring here of the Australian Research Council (Linkage Grant) and the Australia Council for the Arts with Faculty of Education and Social Work (The University of Sydney). Chief Investigators, Professor Andrew Martin, Associate Professor Michael Anderson and Dr. Robyn Gibson are investigating the role of arts education in school students' academic motivation, engagement, and achievement. This research follows on from the US-based *Champions of Change* research.

7 Teaching Knowledge and Skills in Drama Education

Debating knowledge

I was recently out to dinner with some friends of mine who had brought some friends of theirs. The night started as these things often do with polite chatter about what you do. 'Yes well, I teach drama education at a university'. The person I was sitting next to worked as a recruiter and kind of nodded with a screwed up face, indicating he had no idea what I did and was not that interested in finding out. Pleasantries were exchanged and the night got a little more raucous as these things do. Just as the main course arrived, which took an age, he turned back and said to me vehemently, 'you know the problem with you buggers in the arts, you just don't teach anyone anything, no facts, nothing tangible that you can hold onto, just feelings and expression'. For some reason, he had become quite angry about all this and my attempts at rational argument went nowhere in particular as he jumped from how much he hated the arts in general to right wing radio commentators that he admired.

In some ways there is nothing particularly remarkable about this encounter over dinner with my new 'friend'. Anyone who has been involved in the arts or taught the arts for longer than five minutes needs to develop an armoury of responses for this kind of attack. The discussion did for me though, crystallized what people think of when they think of knowledge in the arts. For drama teachers, the challenge then becomes how we might turn this argument on its head. Given the chance the argument I would have made to the recruiter was drama has a strong, vibrant and dynamic knowledge base . As Goethe[1] argues 'Knowing is not enough; we must apply. Willing is not enough; we must do'. In this chapter, I will outline some of the knowledge that is foundational to drama and pick up on one of the themes introduced in Chapter One about drama being the model for productive pedagogy.

Knowledge and skills in drama education

While this chapter presents some cases and engages in some 'how to' approaches, it will mainly review the research and practice of teaching knowledge and skills in drama. That said, it will not and cannot divorce content from process and you will notice many of the themes developed in earlier chapters emerging as we discuss the content of drama education. Let us first discuss why drama has a substantial claim to call itself the productive pedagogy.

Towards more effective teaching

The research literature attests that effective teachers make a difference in student learning (Hayes et al., 2006, p. 1). If we believe that we as teachers have a significant role in the outcomes of our students, the quality of our teaching will be paramount. One of the ways that new teachers can understand pedagogy is through a systematic framework such as the productive pedagogy model. As much as this chapter features this approach, I would like first to describe briefly the context and meaning of this model for drama teachers. The term has appeared under various guises including (but not limited to) *Authentic Pedagogies* (Newmann et al., 1996), *Productive Pedagogies* (Education Queensland, EQ, 2000) and the *NSW Quality Teaching Framework* (NSW DET, 2003). This framework identified three dimensions that are the central pillars of the model. They are

(i) Intellectual quality
(ii) Quality learning environment
(iii) Significance

EQ argued (2000) that the model should conform to three criteria. They said the model should:

- have meaning in *real* classrooms
- be able to be *sustained* organizationally by schools
- have demonstrated effects on learning outcomes for *all* students.

The framework was an attempt to create a model that identified what effective teachers do, based on evidence and sought to make that explicit so that teaching might become more effective for all teachers in all places. While there have been several iterations of this model, I am going to use the New South Wales version as I think it outlines the approach most clearly.

As Figure 7.1 illustrates, at the centre of the model is intellectual quality learnt and taught through a quality learning environment that is significant to students. Table 7.1 provides some more descriptors of what each of these terms means in practice.

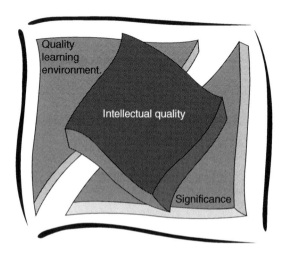

Figure 7.1 The quality teaching framework

	Intellectual Quality	Quality Learning Environment	Significance
Elements	Deep knowlege	Explicit quality criteria	Background
	Deep understanding	Engagement	Knowledge
	Problematic	High expectations	Cultural knowledge
	Knowledge	Social support	Knowledge
	Higher-order thinking	Students' self-regulation	Integration
	Metalanguage	Student direction	Inclusivity
	Substantive		Connectedness
	Communication		Narrative

Table 7.1 The dimensions and elements of the New South Wales quality teaching model

Drama: the productive pedagogy

A drama teacher casting a cursory glance at the Table 7.1 will likely identify these qualities with good drama teaching. I dare say all teachers might see their own practice here, but drama education seems to fit almost all of these descriptors. Other drama educators have also claimed that drama education is highly correlated to this approach. Julie Martello is a leading early childhood drama educator and has consistently advocated drama as a natural fit for a new focus on pedagogical renewal. She argues that:

> many of the criteria for productive pedagogy can be met in just one drama lesson. At the very least these and other successful drama experiences achieve Intellectual Quality through deep under-standing and substantive conversations, they achieve *Relevance* by using real-world problems and drawing on students' background knowledge, they provide *Supportive Environments* by engaging students' interest and integrating every aspect of the work into a meaningful *Narrative* structure. It should not be difficult to position drama at the centre of current dominant discourses by providing further examples of drama as a highly productive pedagogy that integrates the use and extension of multiliteracies. (Martello, 2004, p. 35)

The connections between the aspirations of those who want real change in teaching practice and drama education are fairly clear. Terms like 'Student direction', 'Narrative' and 'Problematic knowledge' are familiar terms to anyone working in drama education. In the remainder of the chapter I would like to outline some of the common areas of drama knowledge or content and apply the concept of productive pedagogies. The intent is to develop a series of approaches to teaching drama knowledge that can also be linked to a systematic, validated method of enhancing pedagogy. The dual aims are not only to connect with what might be considered effective drama practice for twenty-first century students and schools, but to also make links outside drama education to a pedagogical approach that has validity beyond the field. John O'Toole emphasizes the need for drama teachers to make the case for drama being the productive pedagogy:

> The possibilities of drama in the schools are only just being discovered by education systems and their masters. As we hurtle into the millennium, in Hong Kong, Japan, Singapore and Australia too, the worlds of corporation and government are beginning to realize that preparedness for change is the biggest challenge facing us and the next generations; to embrace creativity and teamwork, designers, artists, musicians and performing arts consultants are in demand and short supply. There's a desperate urge to find people who can hypothesise (in other words, can think 'as one of the most basic of drama's catchphrases), empathise, think laterally, make fictional models of possible realities and communicate them to others – all the core business of drama. (O'Toole, 2002)

The argument made by O'Toole and Martello situates drama as a subject that should be at the centre of the curriculum. While drama does enjoy some space in many curricula, it is not near the centre. The remainder of this chapter looks at ways that teachers might engage with drama knowledge effectively creating highly effective practice that will justify itself in any curriculum. We begin with one of the fundamentals, role.

Exploring role

Most drama syllabuses and curriculums throughout the world place role at or near the centre of what they do. Role has come to be understood rather uniquely in drama, and has to some extent drifted from the standard definitions of role. The *Oxford English Dictionary* (2006) defines role as 'the function performed by someone or something in a particular situation or process. Freq. in *to play a role* (*in*)'. Drama education has in practice assumed some of this definition, but shaped it a little more to its purposes. In my experience as a teacher and a researcher in classrooms, role is the presentation of an attitude or a primary motivation. As Haseman and O'Toole (1986) describe it there are three components to role:

- purpose
- status
- attitude.

An understanding of role gives students the beginnings of making imagination three-dimensional as they take on an attitude that can be developed later into a more complex character. In its simplest form, however, it is the demonstration of one aspect of a potentially more complex character. We see roles evident in theatre in the stock characters of the *Commedia dell'arte* including *Il Dottore* (the doctor) who is a caricature of learning – pompous and fraudulent or *Il Capitano* (the captain), a caricature of the professional soldier – swaggering, and cowardly. In these characters, the role is clear. Commedia is popular with younger students because these roles are relatively simple to inhabit. It also explains to some extent why television sitcoms are often imitated by students in class because the roles are relatively simple to reproduce.

When students begin work in role, teachers should intervene to ensure that students are pushed beyond stereotypes to create roles that have integrity even if they are simply rendered. While we are discussing the teacher's role it might be worth touching on an area that has received a great deal of discussion in drama education, the Heathcotian technique which originated[2] in the 1980s of 'teacher in role' or TIR introduced in Chapter Three. John O'Toole et al. (2009) describes how TIR emerged and was received by different teachers he says: 'Thousands of early childhood teachers have naturally, unwittingly, used this convention – that makes many secondary teachers giddily anxious to contemplate – joining the children's dramatic play episodes as a co-player, or teaching maths by setting up shops . . .' (p. 103).

This approach bears some discussion here as there has been a recent resurgence in its popularity among educators. The Mantle of the Expert movement describes the approach as 'A dramatic-inquiry approach to teaching and learning'[3]. Mantle of the expert or poetics of the expert is a strategy within teacher in role that casts the students as the experts in the drama and sees the teacher taking on a lower status role. The core elements of the 'Mantle of the Expert' approach to education appear in Box 7.1.

7.1 Core elements of the 'Mantle of the Expert' approach to education

1. Learners gradually take on responsibility for running an enterprise in a fictional world
2. Learners care enough about the long-term goals of a fictional client that they engage in activities through which they begin to imagine the fictional world
3. Learners and teacher together:
   a. interact predominantly as 'themselves'
   b. imagine that they are interacting as experts who run the enterprise
   c. imagine they are interacting as other people in the world with whom the experts are concerned
4. Over time, the pupils engage in activities that at the same time are both curriculum tasks and that would be professional practices in the fictional enterprise
5. The teacher must share power to position the students (individually and collectively) as knowledgeable and competent colleagues and also ensure that children position one another similarly
6. The children must reflect to make meaning.

Adapted from:
Heathcote, D., and Bolton, G. (1995). *Drama for Learning: Dorothy Heathcote's Mantle of the Expert Approach to Education.* Portsmouth, NH: Heinemann.

There are some strong opinions in drama education about teacher in role approaches. In my practice as a drama teacher, I found it particularly useful as a way to engage with a new idea or a new topic with students up to around 14 years of age. For me, the question of whether to use teacher in role comes down to its fit for the intended learning. Does teacher in role meet the needs of whatever you are teaching? If it is a useful technique, it should be used like any other: if not find another approach.

The danger in role, of course (whether it is a teacher or student taking them on), is that one person's simplistic portrayal is another person's stereotype. Students who engage with role will often go for racist, sexist or ageist roles. As Helen Nicholson reflecting on her own teaching says (1995, p. 17): 'Far from being a gender-neutral activity, children use the context of dramatic playing to become increasingly confirmed in the sex-stereotyped patterns of behaviour . . . . I often felt that young people were constrained by a narrow and culturally defined display of gender roles'. If we go in understanding the dangers inherent in the approach, we are likely to create learning that can deepen understanding of what it is to make an idea three dimensional. As students develop their skills further in taking and developing role they are beginning to act.

Acting

The role of learning about acting has had an odd relationship with drama education over the years. As mentioned in Chapter Three, acting had no place in the classroom for some drama teachers. As Gavin Bolton sees it, this was a relic of the progressivist approach to education. He says, 'As teachers entered the 70s, the emphasis on drama as training in acting had virtually disappeared, but it had been replaced by equally damaging misconceptions: Pupils were encouraged to see drama as a story line, teachers were encouraged to train children through a shopping list of exercises in life skills such as sensitivity and concentration, and the importance of individual activity and self-expression were stressed in the name of progressive education' (Bolton, 1985, p. 153).

If as a drama educator, you accept the place of acting in drama as a valid part of the aesthetic, it will be a central part of your approach to teaching. Much teaching in drama is devoted to controlling the craft of acting and in that sense, it is a central part of controlling the aesthetics of the form. There have been whole libraries devoted to teaching acting and I am not going to even attempt to match wits with Meyerhold, Brook, Stanislavsky or Boal. But I think it might be worth discussing briefly how teachers might structure the teaching of acting to create aesthetic control and aesthetic understanding.

The world of the play: characters in context

Perhaps the first consideration is alerting students that acting only makes sense in the context of its theatrical world. Thus the way students learn to act in a Shakesperean tragedy differs from a modern Verbatim performance like *The Laramie Project*. Understanding the style or form is perhaps the best way into understanding how to act.

The actor-audience relationship

The second key relationship is the actor's connection and understanding of the audience. When building a relationship with the audience, it is worth stressing the importance of creating a clear intention for the audience. A clear intention means that the audience should be in no doubt that the actor has considered the audience when developing their performance[4]. Students should develop the skill of taking the point-of view of the audience member whenever possible and being able to alter their performance to generate different responses from the audience.

Performance skills and characterization

For students the next steps involve:

    (i) understanding of how the *performance skills* of voice, movement and timing might work together
    (ii) create an *authentic character*.

Performance skills such as movement and acting are the essential building blocks for character. In my classroom, I work with performance skills and character so that they are taught and hopefully understood in an integrated way. This is also a way I have found useful to structure my teaching and assessment of acting and characterization.

Exploratory drama: improvisation to playbuilding

I would not be the first person to claim teaching as an improvisation skill. For drama teachers, however Kathleen Gallagher's (2010, p. 46), memories of improvisation's being an essentially 'competitive, male-dominated, derivative theatre form', basically comic in nature, describes what poor improvisation can become. Perhaps the re-orientation that has occurred in the understanding of how improvisation might be useful as a creative and social tool should become the cornerstone of the classroom improvisation experience. Peter O'Connor's Applied Theatre Consultants, who I referred to earlier, uses improvisational techniques to engage audiences and participants in social change. The *Everyday Theatre* program mentioned earlier engages participants in discussions around family violence. It was analysed recently by Viv Aitken (2009). 'The Family Game' uses a semi-structured drama and draws participants in through teacher in role and other improvised techniques to engage with the issues. This kind of structure provides a place for the drama to go, it provides a reason for the improvisation and perhaps most importantly, it represents the ambitions of many for the approach. As Gallagher explains:

> One has the impression that improvisation in educational contexts has come a very long way from the frivolity and distinct lack of structure of its early years. It is now more ambitious about its goals for social transformation and less apologetic about its exploitation of theatre in order to effect such change. (2010, p. 46)

While Peter O'Connor's approach relies on trained actor/teachers presenting a series of 'special improvisations', his work provides a glimpse of how useful improvisation might be for drama classrooms. This approach allows O'Connor and his team to explore these sensitive issues in a safe and supportive way for the students involved. When I have observed this work, what strikes me is the essential paradox of working in improvised forms: structured engagement leads to more effective learning. This observation is based on my reflections on excellent and poor teaching practices using improvisation. It seems the structures create a set of rules that bind and guide the improvisation rather than the old fashioned, rather chaotic approach where 'anything goes'. Teachers seem to fear that they will in some way be seen as directing their students and not allowing sufficient space for their own imaginations and creativity. This is an understandable anxiety; however, the opposite reaction is also deeply problematic. This leads to the 'set and forget' approach where students are left on their own, after an initial brief facilitation' by the teacher, to develop their improvisations. Our role as drama educators is to actively support and at times intervene to foster the development of students as they engage with the dramatic aesthetic. While student-developed work must of course emerge from students themselves, the drama teacher's role is often to structure and restructure the drama as it progresses.

Devising theatre: collaborative playbuilding

This leads fairly naturally to playbuilding in drama. The structures and processes established during the improvisation process should transfer into the students' own playbuilding work. I have found the following approach useful in moving students from the initiation of a topic to the process of making an idea into theatre, in a sense making something one dimensional three dimensional.

Stage 1 Use a dramatic stimulus

The improvisation processes described above provides one approach to developing a play with a group of students. There are many other ways such as pre-text (O'Neill, 1995) that are equally valuable. Whatever approach is chosen, it needs to have the potential to unbundle layers of meaning as the drama progresses. The more the potential, the stimulus has for dramatic tension and has inherent layers of meaning, the richer the playbuilding process is likely to be.

Stage 2 Define the world of the drama

Too often hours of classroom time are whittled away on students who do not really know where they are going with their performances. The 'anything goes' approach identified earlier is at its core anti-dramatic. Drama is an aesthetic with structures and rules, and as students grow in their understanding of the aesthetic, they will become increasingly aware that the structures and conventions in drama create the form of the play. The world of the drama I have described here creates the boundaries of content and form within which the drama will be developed. It may be that students decide to use Brechtian techniques in their devised works including audience distancing and the use of songs to create their play. In addition, they should be able to describe in one sentence the intention of the play or provide a rationale, such as, 'this play will provoke the audience to consider which relationships matter most to them'. Once the world of the drama is defined, everything can and probably will change, but these boundaries will provide students with a clear set of approaches, informed by the aesthetics of drama to work within.

Stage 3: Take control of the aesthetic

The elements of drama are the starting points for controlling the aesthetic. The manipulation of these elements allows the drama to be changed to enhance the student's aesthetic control. If students are able to respond using their understanding of the elements, they are beginning the process of manipulating, altering and refining their dramatic work to make it connect and engage audiences. Some syllabus or curriculum documents refer to this as 'exploring different interpretations of the work' or 'experimenting with conventions'. The terms are more or less interchangeable with experimenting with form and conventions to control the aesthetic. At its simplest level, this process is about students making choices to control the presentation of dramatic meaning for an audience.

Stage 4: Audiences as editors

A critical yet receptive audience that has an understanding of dramatic form should be what we are aiming for in our students when they are the audience. This is the case in the professional theatre or the work of their peers. They should be able to respond in a critical manner and provide informed responses that relate to dramatic elements and form. This approach will provide a powerful motivation for students to hone their devised playbuilding performances. This does not happen accidentally. As I discuss in appreciating drama later in this chapter, students' responses, like their creative work, require structure and discipline. Of course, these responses are only useful if the devisers are able to process and integrate this feedback to make their performances more effective and that skill also needs to be structured.

Writing drama

Plays and playwriting have the capacity to illuminate and challenge our experiences and understandings of culture. Allowing students to inhabit and share this uniquely personal space empowers them with transformative pathways and informs them with choice (Boal, 2000). Through playwriting, students gain a sense of themselves as interpreters of and contributors to their world. As Chizhik argues: 'Playwriting can . . . build strong connections between what is taught in school with what is culturally practiced in urban communities outside of school' (2009, p. 388).

Recent research (Dupré, 2006; Chizhik, 2009; Baroski, 2009) provides evidence that playwriting programs can have strong benefits for student literacy, confidence and creativity, especially for those in margainalized environments. Apart from bringing into focus key writing skills, like story structure, sentence construction, spelling and reading, Chizhik (2009) found students acquiring confidence and self-esteem both in regard to applying those skills from playwriting across other standardized texts.

According to the research, there are several benefits apparent when playwriting is introduced into learning programs. Chizik argues that it is these benefits '. . . when developed, that provide the foundation for transference of literacy skills from the context of playwriting to standardized tests of writing' (2009, p. 392). He discusses four levels of creative engagement embedded in the playwriting process:

1. analysing whether the written words communicate intended thoughts;
2. re-creating or re-imagining experiences to communicate their work;

3. employing practical problem-solving skills, as they endeavour '. . . to mould their ideas into the structural requirements of the play' (Salavante in Chizhik, 2009, p. 389).
4. enlisting their own experiences and world-view within their play's content thus reinforcing their self-esteem and their willingness to communicate.

Enabling students to share their voices to engender deeper understandings of themselves and others is a significant outcome of Dupré's (2006) research into creative drama and playwriting, which focused on tolerance and conflict resolution strategies in her language arts classes. She argues, 'Promoting tolerance through . . . writing reflective journals and plays, among other curricular activities, presented me with opportunities to engage students in a dialogue that honoured their own cultural diversity while encouraging awareness and acceptance of the culture of their classmates' (Dupré, 2006, p. 7).

Recent research (Baroski, 2009) indicates that playwriting offers students opportunities to develop new ways of communicating that explore difference, renegotiate stereotypes and create new narratives of the self and 'the other'. Playwriting goes beyond developing understandings of composition and writing alone; it is able 'to contribute to a healthy interrogation of issues and topics of concern to the group' (McKean, 2007, p. 504). As drama tells stories embedded in relationship, crisis and emotion, students develop awareness that their work is both interpretative and dynamic. Plays navigate conflict moment to moment on multiple levels, from what is happening in the character's outer world to its impact on inner worlds. So plays engage not through conflict alone, but how the characters deal with it, the choices they make and the perceptions they have (McKean, 2007). The characters negotiations with their shifting realities in the play 'allows the audience to draw conclusions from what the characters say and do rather than just have them say it directly' (Wright, 1997, p. 16).

The process of writing plays for students revisits the balance between aesthetic control and aesthetic understanding. Students must first understand the processes involved in scripted drama. How the playwright works with research, workshops the developing play with actors and so on and how these processes end up as the written text. In other words, how does the playwright choose from the 'available designs' (NLG, 1996) when creating the dramatic text. Having made discoveries here, the student is then able to create her own plays using a now broadened understanding of the process and the available designs in the creation process.

Working with scripted drama

As you may have deduced by now at the top of a list called 'what not to do in a drama classroom', the unprepared reading of scripts around the room would come first for me. When I think back on my own experience as a teacher and a student, the cold reading of scripts would be for me perhaps the most destructive pedagogical practice around. As Hankey (2005) argues in their preface to *Othello*: 'A play is much more than words on a page. The text itself is no more than a sketch, an unfinished picture. At every turn it poses hundreds of questions which can only ever be answered by actor, designer or director, in practice upon a stage' (2005, p. v). The response by teachers who want to make young people alive to the power of drama is to engage in whatever way possible in the classroom with the immediacy and dynamism of live performance.

Enter the contextual world of the drama

It is obvious to anyone familiar with theatre that all drama comes from a time and a place. This is not always obvious to our students. In my experience, unless asked to consider the social, contextual and historical contexts, some students are not inclined to give it a second thought. The context of the drama is essential to understanding the way the aesthetics are crafted to engage with the intentions of the playwright and the ways the work might be staged today. Another aspect of this contextual world is understanding how the playwright's, crafting of the play and how productions of the work (including design, direction, acting and set) combine to create the meaning of the play for an audience.

Start with the dramatic tension

After trying many different approaches to teaching *Romeo and Juliet* that foundered as soon as students began struggling in vain with the demands of Shakesperean language, I decided to try something new (for me). By going to the heart of the drama, that is the plays dramatic tension teachers can uncover the essential element that engages the audience. So instead of beginning the study of *R and J* by trawling through Elizabethan theatre history or reading around the room, I started with a pretext for my 14-year-old students. My introduction to the play went something like:

> So there are two teenagers, let's call them Rhouba and Dan. They are both 14 and are both madly in love. Great. But their families are involved in a bitter and violent dispute and have forbidden them from seeing each other. They need to be together but they can't . . . what do you think happens next?

This is not nearly as well written as:

> Two households, both alike in dignity,
> In fair Verona, where we lay our scene,
> From ancient grudge break to new mutiny,
> Where civil blood makes civil hands unclean.
> From forth the fatal loins of these two foes
> A pair of star-cross'd lovers take their life;
> Whole misadventured piteous overthrows
> Do with their death bury their parents' strife.
> The fearful passage of their death-mark'd love,
> And the continuance of their parents' rage,
> Which, but their children's end, nought could remove,
> Is now the two hours' traffic of our stage;
> The which if you with patient ears attend,
> What here shall miss, our toil shall strive to mend.

Of course I am trying to connect the students' lived experience to their learning to engage them in the relevance of this work for their lives. From this, the whole play can be understood through processes such as a *whoosh* where the story of the play is read and students take on the roles improvising the dramatic action of the play. This takes around two minutes, but provides a 'way in' that is engaging before they see one word of Elizabethan text.

Engage in the text

When the time does come to engage with the text, I usually select a small amount of text to help students begin. These excerpts are read as students walk around the room individually and then performed (script in hand) including movement and blocking. Working with the text in this way ensures that students understand it as performance first and begin the process of wrestling with controlling it as a theatrical presentation.

So for instance for Romeo:

She speaks:

> O, speak again, bright angel! for thou art
>
> As glorious to this night, being o'er my head
>
> As is a winged messenger of heaven
>
> Unto the white-upturned wondering eyes
>
> Of mortals that fall back to gaze on him
>
> When he bestrides the lazy-pacing clouds
>
> And sails upon the bosom of the air.

Or Juliet

> Tis but thy name that is my enemy;
>
> Thou art thyself, though not a Montague.
>
> What's Montague? it is nor hand, nor foot,
>
> Nor arm, nor face, nor any other part
>
> Belonging to a man. O, be some other name!
>
> What's in a name? that which we call a rose
>
> By any other name would smell as sweet;
>
> So Romeo would, were he not Romeo call'd,
>
> Retain that dear perfection which he owes
>
> Without that title. Romeo, doff thy name,
>
> And for that name which is no part of thee
>
> Take all myself.

While there is still a fair bit for 12- or 14-year-olds to deal with in the language, here they are handling a contextualized piece of text as a performance, making the future explorations of this work potentially more accessible and more satisfying than the read around the class approach.

Engage in the drama

When students have become more confident with the text, moving to short scene work helps them to grapple further with this work in performance. During the work on these scenes, I encourage a spirit of experimentation rather than a preoccupation with 'getting the right reading'. The sooner students understand that drama has an interpretative flexibility, the sooner they will play with the dynamism of the dramatic form.

Throughout all these processes, the teacher should intervene as much as required to support the drama learning and to help students theatrically explore the text. At all times, there is an attempt to create a high quality learning environment that is significant and relevant to students and strives for intellectual quality in the exploration of drama as performance first and foremost.

As with the other approaches listed here, there is obviously more to say and in truth, discussions of pedagogy around these areas could and in some cases have spawned whole books. In the end, the distinctive nature of this art form is its liveness and its ability to physicalize ideas on stage. As Helen Nicholson so elegantly puts it:

> All dramatic practices, whether they are educational, community-based or created for professional theatre, rely on a synthesis of memory and invention. Live performance, however the term 'performance' is understood, depends on an uncertain mix of the known and the unpredictable, created in the encounters between participants, actors and audiences in the immediacy of the performative moment [2009].

If we, as teachers, keep that aspiration at the centre of our pedagogy, the dynamism and excitement of drama will be infectious in our classrooms.

Dramatic forms: Verbatim Theatre

In many syllabuses, students are asked to engage with dramatic forms. I thought we might discuss the background to a currently popular form and then discuss how it might be approached in the classroom. Evolving from documentary theatre in the mid-1960s, Verbatim Theatre takes taped interviews and oral accounts as its primary source material (Paget, 1987, p. 317). Capturing the uniqueness of individuals' stories; it both informs and engages an audience by interweaving different perspectives of often the same event. Developed for specific communities in regional Britain, Verbatim plays provided a platform for the silent or marginalized in that community. Their voices could be heard for the first time in a framework and vernacular endemic to place; fixed in a locale, the text inspired relatedness and identity.

Memories, typically free from analysis, raw and vivid, were gathered through interviews. These hours of tapes were then transcribed, edited and frequently fed back into the community as a play by the same actors, who first collected the stories, as a way of triangulating the data. The theatre projects that came out of this process represented a way of understanding a shared past, a traumatic present, a diversity of truths. Verbatim Theatre provided a forum for debate by exposing similarities and differences; its purpose was to reveal truths in a simple and accessible way through authentic personal narratives.

When approaching a dramatic form as an opportunity for learning, it is worth analysing the potential for making and appreciating within the form. I have chosen to discuss Verbatim theatre here because the technique is prominent in the form through its reliance on the verbatim testimony of real people in real situations. The shift from 'pure Verbatim' approaches to the approach now favoured by writers such as David Hare[5] is in itself fertile ground for debate and discussion when teaching the form. The approach or methodology gives students the opportunity to examine the work of a Verbatim theatre maker such as Moises Kauffman or perhaps David Hare and based on the study of their work and their approaches build their own Verbatim piece. Again students in this approach are not only learning 'about' Verbatim; they are learning 'to (do)' Verbatim, enriching the potential for learning about the form. And though this approach is viable for most dramatic styles or forms, it is just a case of developing learning that exploits the experiential potential of the form.

Writing about drama: building a bridge to critical evaluation in drama education

A critical appreciation of drama is crucial to students creating a deep and enduring understanding of the art form. While writing about drama is central to almost all curriculum and syllabus models around the world, there is sometimes a tendency to borrow critical response models from other fields of learning that do not always suit the needs of the subject area. In my experience, drama education has used the models most suited for literature criticism instead of an approach that bridges experiential learning with written analysis. For example, if your students are writing a critical response to *Hamlet*, it is crucial for their understanding of drama that they understood how Shakespeare created meaning through the staging and the text, not just the text alone. Students in drama should be able to use evidence from their experience of the play in their critical responses.

Experiential work

At this stage, students through workshops and other practical activities should be experiencing the text and exploring its theatrical potential to make meaning. Students during this stage should be noticing how the elements of drama interact to produce a theatrical statement. At this stage, students should be noticing the performance and theatrical elements but also be mindful of the social and cultural context of the play. If you were exploring *Three Sisters* by

Anton Checkov, you would work with the text, encouraging students to perform extracts from it, and discuss the design issues that are central to its performance. While this process is underway it may be useful to get students to reflect in writing on their discoveries.

Written reflection

The bridge from the experiential to written work should involve reflection on the process and on the social and cultural circumstances that impacted upon and moulded the dramatic work. Students, having worked with the text or topic theatrically, will now be able to use the written reflections as the basis for their written response. These reflections should not only involve 'seeing the play'. They should include their experience of the play. The following response reflects the standard of response required in this type of reflection for instance

> We began the play with pristine costumes. As the play continued, our costumes become more dishevelled suggesting the general theme of decay that is at the heart of the dramatic meaning of the play.

The written response draws on the detail of the play and practitioner to make points that answer the question. It may be useful during the year to provide students with specific and general questions so they have a chance to respond to both.

Students should develop skills in responding to broad questions, using their knowledge of the playtexts and their performance of them from their experiential learning. Students who recognize the relationship between the socio-cultural and the performance and theatrical aspects of the plays and use their experiences to mould their responses, will begin to develop a critical understanding that reflects their immersion in the art form.

Evaluating presentations: getting beyond 'I like it'

Teaching students to become critical and reflective audiences is one of the keys to creating a drama classroom with intellectual quality. As discussed throughout this book, a performance, whether it be professional or in schools, still requires feedback. In the drama education classroom, an audience is far more active than those found generally in theatre. In my ideal classroom where students are engaged in the process, I envisage them wandering around the performance changing their view as their interest takes them so they can create multiple perspectives. This approach is perhaps more akin to the spect-actorship described earlier that Boal envisages (2000). Spect-actors are active in the drama and often take the place of the actor to show a different approach. The spect-actor seems far more appropriate to the needs of the developing and sometimes improvised work than the passive audience who are disconnected from the drama by the invisible 'fourth wall'.

The feedback from the audience is the way performers can change their approach to enhance their connection with their audience. So some, guidance may be required for students to become effective audiences. Beyond the superficial 'I like that', 'I didn't like that',

Table 7.2 Pavis McAuley questionnaire

Plot	Space of performance
Story	Audience scenography
Structure	Lighting
Characters	Music, sound fx
Themes	Props
Motifs	Costumes
Language (including register and tone)	Director
Imagery and symbols	Actors
Genre	Focus
Gender issues	Proxemics
Socio-political context	Pace/tempo changes
Ideological position	

or 'I was bored', deep and useful evaluation goes to the heart of why a particular perform-ance *worked* or didn't work. A useful approach to structure feedback is providing stu-dents with the elements of drama and ask them to respond on one or two of the elements and then make a comment on the performance as a whole. These discussions should be critical but supportive. The same approach (perhaps minus the wandering) can be applied to the professional theatre. In this context, the theatrical space, design and the direction are more likely to feature in student evaluations. The Pavis McAuley checklist (McAuley, 2000) which is derived from semiotic analysis provides one approach to discussing profes-sional performances. The checklist, Table 7.2 uses familiar categories to prompt student responses.

Written reflection is a time-honoured way to discuss drama and theatre. The traditions of theatrical criticism and performance studies have provided ways for theatre to be under-stood beyond the context of the actual production. Effective written reflection in the drama classroom will reflect the characteristics of these traditions and feature critical engagement, a sense of the live performance experience, an understanding of the context and a discus-sion of how dramatic meaning is created theatrically.

Conclusions

The intention of this chapter, indeed this book, is to provide ways teachers might concep-tualize drama knowledge. Drama knowledge is physical, experiential and cerebral in ways that are distinctive in the arts, schooling and society. It is founded in pedagogical effective-ness. The productive pedagogies model that features intellectual quality, quality learning environment and significance is suited well to teaching the knowledge and skills of drama.

The specific examples here are an attempt to make the case for drama knowledge and its potential to provide something unique to a young person's journey in education. Goethe's quote 'Knowing is not enough; we must apply. Willing is not enough; we must do' goes a long way to summing up what knowledge in a drama classroom actually entails. Knowledge here is physical, it is applied to a dramatic problem and it is responsive to the dynamics of the aesthetic that are ultimately reflective of the human experience.

Notes

1 Johann Wolfgang von Goethe (1832) was a German playwright, poet, novelist and dramatist who lived from 1749 to 1832.

2 John O'Toole claimed (2009, p. 103) that Norah Morgan in fact originated the technique in the 1940s young Canadian Air force officers and was also common in Theatre in Education productions. Even if Heathcote was not the first to use it, she was undoubtedly the first to make the approach popular in education.

3 See www.mantleoftheexpert.com/about-moe/resources/6-key-resources/ for more details. Accessed on 29 Novemeber 2010.

4 This might range from actively engaging them to ignoring the audience depending on the style or form of the piece.

5 David Hare is now using real life events and sometimes testimony to develop his works. They are not strictly speaking Verbatim.

8 Assessing Drama Learning

I have a confession to make. I have always tried to avoid assessment. As an education student at university, I remember thinking how oppressive, anti-intellectual and anti-creative the whole thing was. Toward the end of my degree, I attended a session by a drama educator on the need for authentic assessment in drama. While this wasn't quite the 'road to Damascus' experience, it did give me a feel for how assessment done well and created with the student in mind can make a difference. Since then, I feel like I have been in an unrelenting struggle between those who want assessment to support and enhance student learning and those who want to use it as a tool for school and teacher accountability. There is in a sense nothing wrong with school accountability, it should be part of what schooling systems do, but recently the impulse to denigrate schools and schooling based on assessment scores seems to have gotten out of hand. My view is that it is time to return to the idea that students are the most important stakeholders in schools and to shift assessment back to its proper role as a support for student learning. In drama, this is possible by creating assessment that matches the knowledge or skill being assessed as closely as possible. This chapter attempts a repositioning of assessment so that it suits the needs of students and the subject and not other agendas.

Throughout this book, I have called for an approach that engaged students in the processes of aesthetic control and aesthetic understanding in the drama classroom. One of the persistent problems for drama educators is the same problem that sometimes arises in curriculum, namely we are stuck with approaches that do not necessarily suit the learning area. By this I mean that we are often faced with pen and paper tests as the primary mode of assessment. Written exams are often a pragmatic response to the issues drama raises for educational measurement. Perhaps it is time drama educators promoted a different way of assessment as the norm that more closely matches our needs. I am thinking here of assessment approaches that measure a student's aesthetic control and aesthetic understanding in what is essentially a collaborative, interactive learning experience. Drama assessment is about nuance and subtlety, and so the traditional high stakes testing regimes that seem to be all the rage currently will not suffice. As Posner argues:

> For real problems, the appropriate methods of attack are not immediately obvious and may well vary greatly from those that apply to problems that seem similar. In contrast, on a standardized test, where there is no time for subtlety or deep analysis, problems are by necessity formulaic. Could an education driven standardized test scores leave students unable to understand such subtleties? (2004, p. 79)

Standardized testing, by its very nature, is a reductionist approach and not particularly useful for much that we do in arts learning, and particularly the nature of learning in drama. When students begin to experiment with role, they are using their bodies, their imagination, often dialogue all at once in a complex interplay that was described earlier by David Wright as a '. . . complex feedback system . . . [that] can generate challenging and unpredictable results' (2005, p. 1).

It is so much easier to assess a static and pervasive product like an essay or a multiple-choice test. These assessment items do not invite the complexity of a transitory performance where assessment decisions need to be made on the spot with little chance of referring back to an artefact (like an exam paper) to double check the assessor's impressions. Pen and paper examinations have their uses (which I will discuss later in this chapter), but they cannot measure authentically the embodied skills that pervade drama education. Drama requires assessment that mirrors the requirements of the learning rather than narrow reporting imperatives that so often drive assessment strategies.

It is perhaps no co-incidence that alongside the rise in external, standardized testing, especially in literacy and numeracy over the last decade, the principles and models of authentic assessment have received renewed attention. Debates about the reliability, validity and utility of assessment instruments to effectively account for what students know, understand and can do, have become increasingly complex as national and international testing regime, and the uses to which the data from these are put, become *de rigueur* on the educational landscape.

These debates about the nature and usefulness of assessment instruments have been particularly vigorous in the creative arts and English curriculum areas, given their philosophical and practical inclusion of the aesthetic and the expressive and these subject emphasis on making, performing and creating. Questions about the function of assessment, and the optimal means of validly measuring student achievement in the arts is inevitably linked to questions about the consonance between the intended curriculum and student outcomes; process and product; and what Eisner has termed 'educational connoisseurship and educational criticism' (Eisner, 2002, p. 187). According to Eisner, when it comes to assessment in the creative arts, 'three features commend themselves:

1. The technical quality of the work produced;
2. The extent to which it displays an inventive use of an idea or process;
3. The expressive power of aesthetic quality it displays'.

I am not arguing that we should be backing away from assessing drama – far from it. My argument is that many of the traditional and to some extent enduring models of assessment that rely exclusively on pen and paper testing are not appropriate for assessment in drama. What is required is a set of assessment approaches that engage authentically with the art form to produce approaches that mirror the skills and knowledge of drama learning rather than rely on assessment practices that have been bequeathed to us from other curricula like English. While sole reliance on pen and paper testing is to be avoided, this kind of response is useful when engaging with appreciation. Student understanding of appreciation in many cases must be expressed through an academic critical mode and a written response allows this kind of response to be assessed efficiently. The problem arises when this is the only way that assessment takes place. Narrow assessment practices also have the tendency to diminish students' aesthetic understanding according to Philip Taylor (2006): 'Most assessment and evaluations fail to take into account the aesthetic dimension. Too many theatre educators are concerned with discrete skill deposits, principally because of the outcomes orientation of most schools . . . the standards era, with its concern for delivering a pre-packaged content and skill kit, has actually deskilled teachers and students' (2006, p. 1).

I am not suggesting here that there are definitive models, but rather there are a set of principles that can be applied to drama learning that will make it fair and productive for our students. Let's turn now to the wider context of assessment in the arts before focussing on my aspirations for assessment suited to learning in drama.

Assessment in the arts

There has been much, often fruitless, discussion about how the arts can be assessed. On the one hand, the subjectivists who argue that art forms cannot bear scrutiny because it is all really in the 'eye of the beholder' plague the arts. The others push for objective summative, testing as seen in the national literacy and numeracy testing. This kind of approach asks students to fit their art within rigid criteria. Both of these extremes present great difficulties for arts education. There is an approach that is tried and tested in the arts that allows a trained subjectivity to be applied to the assessment of art works and for our purposes drama. 'Trained subjectivity' (Thompson, 1991, p. 77) accepts that drama teachers (and assessors) come with an understanding and experience of drama and theatre from their lives as teachers and audiences. Rather than seeing this as some kind of inhibition to effective assessment, this subjectivity or experience is prized. The next step is to train those assessing drama through discussion and moderation practices to ensure that valid criteria can frame effectively the subjectivity of the teacher. I am not arguing here that any of us can claim objectivity in any of our assessment practices, but rather that we should prize our subjectivity (which comprises knowledge and experience) and strive with other skilled educators in assessment to come to a common understanding using common but flexible criteria. The following principles frame the development of assessment in drama.

Five principles of effective drama assessment

Later in this chapter, we will discuss specific approaches to assessment in drama learning, but these principles underpin an effective approach to assessment in drama learning. This approach draws from a broad spectrum of assessment and learning theory to construct an approach that provides authentic assessment constructively aligned to drama learning.

Drama learning assessment should be authentic and relevant to the art form

Unlike other areas of education, drama learning not only has an aesthetic to measure itself against, but also has a dynamic and thriving professional art form to consider. Assessment in this area should in this sense have one eye on that relationship with the industry and the innovation occurring there, and one eye on the aesthetics of drama (which are obviously interrelated). This provides a wonderful opportunity for drama educators to develop assessments that borrow from professional theatre in forms of authentic assessment that Wiggins (1993, p. 229) says engages students in '. . . worthy problems or questions of importance, in which students must use knowledge to fashion performances effectively and creatively. The tasks are either replicas of or analogous to the kinds of problems faced by adult citizens and professionals in the field'. While there is nothing particularly new about authentic assessment, it does allow drama educators to make a case for their learning area based on its relationship to one of the oldest cultural industries: drama and theatre. The necessary caveat here is that drama education is not and can never be the same as the theatre industry. Carroll's argument about the link between film learning and the film industry is also true for drama: 'A professional craft-based model produces a particular form of film, which cannot be reproduced in classroom environments because its very nature demands time, energy and skill to the exclusion of any other curriculum concern . . . the expense in time and effort is often too high for secondary curriculum-based schools to sustain' (2008, p. 182).

When designing drama assessment approaches, teachers should be guided by the learning needs of the students, not only the nature of the industry. Schools do not have the resources nor can they justify making classrooms mini professional theatre companies or theatre training centres. Drama learning should rather be a place where the best of the theatre industry can be employed to support the learning and assessment aims of the drama classroom. Borrowing practices and adapting them for learning is commonplace in music, film and design based curriculum. The implications for drama learning are that we must strive to align the learning with the skill or understanding being taught. If we want to assess a critical response to a drama, a written essay response is appropriate. If we wish to assess improvisation skills an improvisation exercise aligns most effectively with the actual learning.

Assessment should be about learning and not only about measurement

The overwhelming legacy of the assessment for learning movement has been the shift away from a narrowly based conception of assessment to incorporating assessment as a learning rather just a measurement tool. One of the strongest proponents of this approach has been Paul Black who has long argued the case for the centrality of formative assessment in the development of student learning. His studies in 1988 and 2004 explored the links between assessment and learning. His research found that there was overwhelming evidence that formative assessment practices are central to the growth and development of student learning. There was however some ambiguity about how formative assessment might be optimized to make learning even more effective for students. I have summarized in Table 8.1 the findings of his 2004 study that makes recommendations for improving assessment practices to enhance learning and noted the implications for drama learning.

Table 8.1 Implications for assessment of drama learning

Assessment for Learning in the Classroom (Black et al., 2004)	Implications for drama learning
Change the 'classroom contract' so that all expect that teacher and students work together for the same end: the improvement of everyone's learning.	Learning in drama should focus on *continuous assessment* that relies on the process and product of drama. The expectations here are for group rather than individual learning. Students are responsible for their peers learning as well as themselves.
Empower students to become active learners, thus taking responsibility for their own learning.	An environment of intellectual and aesthetic curiosity should be established to promote active and responsible learning as the tasks become more *learner centred*.
Incorporate changes in the teacher's role one step at a time, as they seem appropriate. Move from 'instructor' to 'facilitator'.	As the teacher is able she should hand over the aesthetic *responsibility to the students* so she becomes less directive in her teaching and more of a support for the learning.
Attention to and reflection on ways in which assessment can support learning.	*Learning should follow the skills* or *understanding being taught.* For instance acting should be assessed on the ability of students to act effectively within the style they have chosen.

The implications here are for a wholesale reorientation of the way learning takes place. For many arts educators this will be consistent with their current practice, for others this approach will be new. For many teachers, the only way for learning to occur is to encourage student engagement with their developing understanding of drama and theatre. For those who already teach in this way, the next important step is to reorient their approach to assessment.

To illustrate this concept, let us suppose that we are developing teaching and assessing the skills of theatrical direction. An approach that develops an assessment for learning will create a seamless alignment with the skill being developed and the assessment of those skills. Assessment here will see students directing actors within the context of a playscript. The formative phase may assess the students understanding of theatrical technology, the design of the work, the layers and subtext of the script. Overall though the assessment will focus on how effectively the student can create theatre on stage that engages an audience with clarity and meaning. In addition, an assessment of the final performance, the finished production will provide a useful stimulus for peer discussion and assessment. In this brief example, we are focusing on the assessment to enhance and not only measure the learning. The integrity of the measurement is undiminished. The measurement is enhanced as it aligns more closely with the learning. Assessment developed in this way enhances drama education by making the assessment a central feature of the learning. It demands that students collaborate to support and assess their peers. This assessment approach can only be successful if it considers making and appreciation as interactive concepts.

Drama learning should assess the appreciating and making of drama and theatre as an interaction rather than a separation

I have argued throughout this book that the arbitrary separation of appreciating and making has done the arts a major disservice. The implications for assessment are that we must develop assessment that reflects the interconnectedness of appreciating and making in drama learning. This approach can be demonstrated by examining the assessment of a student-devised drama. A large part of student performance is drawn from scripts developed by playwrights. There is however, in many drama curricula internationally, an equal focus on student self-devised work (O'Toole et al., 2009). When students are learning the making processes of self-devising, it is useful for them to appreciate the work of professional theatre devisers such as Mike Leigh. In 2006, Mike Leigh produced *Two Thousand Years* for the National Theatre in London. The play, like many of his other works, revolves around the daily lives of 'ordinary characters'. In *Two Thousand Years* he reflects somewhat autobiographically on his Jewish roots. Mike Leigh devises theatre with an ensemble allowing the characters to unfold as he works with them rather than the more traditional work with an existing text. He described his approach to devising film and theatre in a recent interview with Chloe Veltman from *Believer* magazine:

> My job apart from anything else is to build an ensemble composed of actors who all come from a
> secure place so that they can all work together to make the film. So on the whole, frankly, trust is

not much of an issue. What I don't do, as you know, is throw actors instantly into a dangerous situation. The actors I select for my projects sit and chew the fat with me for ages before we gradually get the characters on the go. So by the time they get to the bit that's dangerous, they've spent a lot of time sorting things out without any pressure. Nobody's watching them but me. We're careful and slow. The reason my films work is because every actor on set is very secure. They're able to fly. (Leigh, 2009)

Leigh's approach to devising provides a strong basis for the development of student's own devising work. After students have appreciated (analysed and discussed) how Leigh creates drama through improvising characters, students can attempt something of the same approach themselves. A short essay detailing Leigh's approach and reflecting on how students might apply this approach to their own work could form the basis of their response. This would allow for the assessment of appreciation and build a bridge to their own devising work. Of course Leigh's level of skill and experience is not at the same as a 14-year-old drama student, but neither is Beethoven's mastery the same as a 14-year-old music student. The point is that through an appreciation we can attempt similar processes. The intention in this learning scenario is that the appreciation of Mike Leigh's approaches supports the students developing understanding of the processes involved in devised work. The devised performance (maximum 10 minutes) could be assessed on the quality of each performer's contribution (to the performed work on stage). The assessment here must tie the analysis in with the making in the same way the learning activities take place. The assessment criteria then focusses on the appreciation (short essay on Mike Leigh's approach) and the product (performance of devised work) to align the learning to assessment and make the link between appreciating and making in drama.

There are potential pitfalls here. There will be students who are not able to create their own devised work and who rely on the work of others unfairly and who create derivative or poor imitations of the inspiration, in this case Mike Leigh. In any approach that relies on appreciation this is a potential danger. A key expectation of this approach is that students develop their own approach influenced but not copied from other theatre makers. The soundest response to this risk is to devise criteria that require the students to be innovative in their approach while using some of the established techniques.

The assessment of drama learning should be achieved through the inclusion of group assessment

A focus on collaborative processes is hardly new, and for decades collaborative learning has been largely uncontroversial. The main instrument is formative assessment that is also now largely uncontroversial but does sit at odds with some of the high stakes testing schemes in place for students of all ages in large Western education systems. Chapters One and Five of this book characterized drama learning as a collaborative experience, as a community of practice that relies on interaction and co-operative learning. While these are not new pedagogies, they do demand a reconceptualization of the often-individualistic approaches to assessment found in secondary schooling. The most common complaint about group assessment approaches is the criticism that they lack integrity because individual achievement is dependent on the interactions of others. This view of collaborative assessment is superficial. It misunderstands the reorientation that arts education demands for learning and consequently assessment. This view is also based on the premise that an individual's contribution to the whole cannot be effectively assessed without other students 'contaminating' the individual's contribution.

The evidence for the effectiveness can be seen in high stakes testing regimes that include group assessment forms. The New South Wales Higher School Certificate is the matriculation examination for students in the largest state (by population) in Australia. In the drama examination, more than 6000 students are examined annually on their ability to devise and perform a group performance, 8–12 minutes duration with 3–6 performers. Students are assessed formatively through classroom-based assessment and summatively on their performances before 2–3 external examiners. These examiners mark against a set of defined criteria and established standards. This process has been in place since 1993. This is one small example, but many other international examples demonstrate how co-operative learning can be rigorously and uncontroversially assessed and can be incorporated into high stakes examinations for university entrance if required.

This approach to assessing collaborative learning (see Table 8.2) has a similar flavour to this example. Students are assessed on the development of a devised work on the basis of the role they take on in the process. For instance, students undertaking set design in a devised drama task[2] have a set of formative and summative criteria applied to their work. The formative assessment could take the form of a portfolio or a seminar on how they plan to develop and use the set in the devised performance. The summative phase of the assessment is the finished product and this has two components. One component provides a mark for the performance on a set of summative criteria; the other half of this mark relates to the performance design specifically, which has its own set of criteria. The assessment schedule is reflected in Table 8.2.

This approach underscores the importance of the collaboration and each individual contribution. In addition, each individual student's contribution to the whole is assessed. What emerges is an assessment approach that more closely reflects the responsibilities of each individual, but does not diminish the importance of the collaboration.

Table 8.2 Assessment schedule devised drama task

Assessment type	Individual role (lighting design, director)	Performance of devised work
Formative weighting	25	25
Summative weighting	25	25

I have not discussed the other learning that is taking place here that may be considered general or tacit learning such as team work skills, development of negotiation skills, problem solving or project management, and so on. I have not separated these competencies out from drama learning, as they are drama learning. Drama learning is learning about negotiation, problem solving and so on. Like the other arts, few teachers believe that all of our students will one day become professional actors or designers. I believe, however, that involvement in collaborative learning such as drama contributes crucially to developing significant life skills such as negotiation and teamwork.

Assessment in drama learning should avoid dichotomies

The long running and ultimately futile argument about the place of process and product in learning and assessment in drama education (Anderson, 2004) and to a lesser extent other areas of arts has no place in modern arts curriculum. This discussion is roughly analogous to the questions that permeate educational assessment relating to whether summative or formative assessment is more appropriate.

The evidence of a meta study of over 250 other studies by Black and William (1998) argues that formative assessment does raise student achievement from early childhood to adulthood. Gillies (2007, p. 190) argues, '. . . there is strong evidence that the use of formative assessment or "assessment for learning" leads to higher quality learning and enhanced learning outcomes'. This is another ultimately futile dichotomy that has had its day. You will have noticed that through this chapter, the examples have drawn from summative and formative assessment approaches. The message is that there is importance in process and product, formative and summative assessment and appreciation and making. While the approaches will be applied in different proportions at different times, the tendency toward a balance is likely to be more effective. The distortions that emerge in curriculum and assessment can be seen everywhere when product based assessment is allowed to override formative assessment of processes. The insidious overtesting of students in the United States, the United Kingdom and Australia demonstrates a system out of balance where learning has become subservient to sometimes meaningless diagnostics. The challenge for drama teachers is to cope with the issues that arise in the assessment of process. While assessing product in drama learning is no simple matter, there is significant skill required for the teacher attempting to assess the subtleties of a collaborative process and provide a rigorous and perceptive assessment task that supports learning. For example, if we set our senior students a task to produce a collaborative devised drama lasting at least five weeks, we need to assess the following in collaborative drama:

- How is the dramatic meaning developed and what contribution does each student make to the whole performance?
- To what extent does each individual incorporate the elements? In other words, how does the set designer or the director contribute to the process and the final product of the drama?
- How does each student contribute to an effective and dramatically meaningful performance?
- To what extent are the conventions of drama taken into account when creating the devised drama?

- How effective is the final product? (The criteria that can be applied to effectiveness are explained later in this chapter).

This is not a checklist, rather it indicates the processes and product that need to be discussed and engaged as part of the dramatic process. The balance between formative and summative assessment reflects well the demands of drama learning, which draw on the process and the product to create a devised performance.

Strategies for drama assessment

These principles provide the underpinnings of what is a sound and authentic approach to drama assessment. In the next section of this chapter are some tangible strategies around these principles by suggesting a coherent assessment strategy that can be used to assess drama learning in the classroom. The following is a scheme for developing drama learning in the classroom. There are two approaches to assessment suggested here. The first is suited to junior high school students and the second supports assessments in the senior years of schooling. The assessments are a mixture of approaches including:

- a graded collaborative project (all members receive the same mark for the completed drama)
- an individual grade based on the students contribution to the collaborative project
- an individual project with an individual mark.

These examples attempt to balance formative and summative assessment of process and product.

Drama project

Age level: 12–14

Outcomes

The student:

1. Uses the development of a character that interacts with other characters to explore an element of human experience.
2. Understands the specific forms and conventions of drama and is able to apply them to the creation of a group devised drama.
3. Appreciates the dramatic techniques and is able to analyse them in their own work and the work of others.
4. Values and understands elements of drama and how they are applied to devised performance.
5. Organizes and presents relevant material relating to the devising of the performance in a clear and coherent manner.

Content

Ensemble devised drama is a way that actors, directors and designers have created drama. Using a case study of a group who work in this way, we will examine their processes and then apply them to our own ensemble devised piece of drama.

Form discussion

Choose a form of drama and a production and look closely at the features of that form. You will need to identify the form's distinctive features and conventions. Write a short response using examples of plays to describe the features of your chosen form. This is worth 20 per cent of the final mark

Building a scene

Develop a scene in your chosen form in small groups. You should use the features and conventions of the form you have identified to build your own scene in groups. The scene should last no longer than 4 minutes. Your final product should include:

- Your performance (4 minutes) (50 per cent)
- An explanation on how your scene meets the requirements of the form (no more than 500 words) (50 per cent).

Assessment task	Description	Weighting/100
Form Discussion	Individually identify a form using examples from productions.	20
Form: scene	Develop a short scene for performance in groups.	60
Form explanation	Individually explain how your scene reflects the form you have chosen.	20

As students become more confident and experienced with collaborative approaches to learning and making, the teacher can allow more autonomous learning to take place. The shift here is from the teacher as director to students devising and producing their own drama. This will not be feasible if they have no experience of the making and appreciating drama.

Playbuilding project

Age level: 15–17

Outcomes

The student:

1. Uses acting and directing skills to communicate dramatically.
2. Uses knowledge and experience of drama to support the development of their own collaborative performance.

⇨

3. Collaborates in the development of the performance.
4. Reflects on the development of the playbuilding process.
5. Values and understands the aesthetics of drama.
6. Engages an audience through an understanding of drama.
7. Synthesizes, organizes and analyses, knowledge, experience and opinion in coherent, informed oral, performed and written responses.
8. Understands the different roles and responsibilities in drama making processes.
9. Works effectively in their specific role in the development of the drama while supporting the overall directorial vision of the drama.

Content

Drama is a collaborative art form. In this collaborative project, students will develop an original collaborative performance (7–10 minutes). All students will negotiate and discuss the project to develop a coherent and effective short drama. Each performance will have a minimum of three and a maximum of five students taking on different roles. Each student will take on one of the following roles in the development of the performance:

- Director
- Designer (Set, Props and Costume)
- Actor/s.

All groups will be assessed in the process of developing their drama on three occasions:

1. the initial ideas
2. dress rehearsal
3. performance.

Group devised performance project

The group devised performance will:

- be a complete aesthetic statement that creates meaning for an audience
- allow each member of the team to contribute to the performance
- be 6–8 minutes in duration.

The group devised performance will be assessed in the following ways:

Assessment task	Description	Weighting/100
Pre-production pitch	The whole group describes in detail the idea for their group devised performance and then individuals describe their approach depending on their role.	25
Production Portfolio	Each student produces a portfolio describing the process of developing their group devised performance focusing on their specific role.	25
Production: individual role	Each student is assessed on how their role contributes to the effectiveness of the performance.	25
Performance	The completed performance is assessed.	25

* Each student individual mark may be moderated against the completed performance.

The teacher will facilitate and support the development of each performance as required. At no time will the teacher or any other outsider (non-student) direct, write or perform any group's work.

This approach is a starting point for those interested in integrating a collaborative approach to group devised performance, but who feel unsure about assessment processes. It recognizes that drama is a collaborative endeavour and values process and product in the production of a final performance. The balance between process and product reflects the value of formative assessment and recognizes a final performance is an essential part of learning in drama. It also values the individual roles/skills as they contribute to the process and product of the performance.

Conclusions

Some may consider this approach to assessment in drama learning radical. This approach moves away from a concentration on appreciation for its own sake and integrates it within the making process and students are assessed on the ways their appreciation supports their making that has been implicit in arts education for decades. The approaches here attempt to strike a balance between making and appreciating and formative and summative assessment. This approach looks first to the drama objectives and then aligns the assessment to it.

I am not pretending that assessment strategies such as these will always be popular with all teachers and they will need to be tailored and changed depending on each schools context. The intent of this approach is to authentically reflect the processes of drama and adapt those processes to schools. There is significant further work to do in developing assessment in drama learning, but these ideas are offered as a way of enlisting assessment in the service of drama learning rather than the other way around.

The next chapter focuses on how teachers can undertake research in their own classrooms to enrich their practice and contribute to the development of more effective theories and practice in drama learning.

Notes

1 I refer here to the traditional large-scale pen and paper, often multiple-choice tests that often control student matriculation. I am not arguing that we should abolish these tests, but rather that they do not always align effectively with learning in arts education.

2 In many approaches to student devising, a student would perform and take another role in the development of the work. For the sake of clarity in this example, I have assumed their only role is set design. Of course this approach could be applied to both roles if required.

Researching Drama Education ⬛**9**

The great research 'adventure'

I remember vividly that moment when I first decided that I could be part of the great research adventure. I would like to say it was a moment when I saw the light of inspiration go on in one of my student's eyes as they understood the potential for drama as a way of knowing for the first time, or perhaps as I saw my students respond to *King Lear* with awe and wonder, but unfortunately it was when I realized qualitative research existed. As a result of this great leap forward, I did not have to do a survey or a statistical manoeuvre like a paired T test in my research. I tell this short story because it sums up the development of drama education research in a way. Many of us were so excited by the possibility of focussing on the quality of the drama learning experience rather than the quantity that we became drama education researchers. The revelation that evidence not only consisted of correlations and statistical significance alone, but patterns of meaning and lived experience opened many drama teachers' eyes to the exciting potential of drama to create qualitative evidence. This chapter is in part a call for research to become a little more multi methodological. I personally feel that qualitative research is the most powerful and exciting place to engage with the big questions and problems in our field. Perhaps in our enthusiasm, however, drama education has failed to develop the diversity of research methods to examine all the challenges that face us and speak to all the audiences that we must convince. Beyond advocacy[1] for drama education, we need a new generation of researchers who can re-examine our taken for granted assumptions and critically explore how we can be more effective educators.

Heathcote's challenge made 20 years ago is still profoundly relevant:

> In drama above all you can't make vague promises . . . When you say something like, 'Drama is good for their language', get rid of it. It doesn't tell anybody how it does it, because it's too vague. 'Drama is good for their personality and all that' – get rid of it because it does a great deal of harm. It doesn't point to what we really have to consider, which is – how does it do it? (Heathcote, 1984, p. 6)

Beyond the vague promises of change that drama education might provide, we are being called more and more to account for our claims by a community of educators who are interested in 'evidence-based practice'. In a world full of claims, how we marshal our resources and state our case is crucial for the maintenance and strengthening of drama's place in the education of the next generation of young people. We are also entering a phase in the history of our subject, as we inch in from the fringes of the curriculum where arts education is being examined with renewed vigour nationally and internationally. The challenge for us is to use that interest to create and sustain a body of research that describes, analyses and advocates our position to many audiences and overcomes new and old challenges. The notion of praxis encourages drama educators to reflect and research their own practice. So much of drama teaching practice is experiential and transient that it may seem to be resistant to 'theoretical capture'. One of the roles of praxis is to capture the practice and provide descriptions and analysis of it using theoretical bases. This chapter makes an argument for teachers finding appropriate and rigorous ways to capture their own practice. It provides some strategies to make research a central part of teacher practice and suggests some of the emerging needs for drama education research.

Telling the research story

When we do research, we are telling a story about our past, reflecting our present and imagining our possible futures. A large part of our imagined future for drama education can only come to pass if we establish and sustain a reflective, viable research base. I imagine a future for drama education that does not separate practice from research. The future I envisage engages research with classroom practice as praxis. For Paulo Freire praxis is at the base of our development as a community. He says 'Liberation is a praxis: the action and reflection of men upon their world in order to transform it . . . . Men are not built in silence, but in words, in work, in action-reflection' (Freire, 1973, pp. 75–6). Friere is calling for the development of a research base that is transformative, liberating, action-based and reflective. In drama learning this takes place as educators join to collaborate on their practice and the learning of their students. My ambition for learning in drama and in schools generally is the same as Friere's – that through reflection and action we might transform our schooling structures to make them more effective and engaging for the young people they serve.

There is another reason teachers involve themselves in research. They are curious about what they have seen in their classroom. In my view, curiosity is the essential precondition for research. Curiosity, creativity and research are linked concepts. Curiosity motivates our students and spurs us to seek responses to those questions that have arisen for us as educators. Sadly, many educators feel unable to go any further than curiosity for lack of resources, time, energy or support. We must find ways to overcome these challenges to justify drama's place in a crowded curriculum. In the midst of rapid social and technological change, research provides a way for us to reform our practices at a micro level (in our own classroom) and gives us some evidence and theory to use at a systemic level.

The looming challenges

As we are all aware, there is currently a generational shift occurring in education. The looming teacher shortages present in schools are upon us in drama education. Many of the established researchers in the area are approaching retirement or have retired, with many to follow in the next decade. We have a limited time to learn from them or miss the opportunity to gain from their immense corporate knowledge. The other change that has taken place is the position of drama in the curriculum. There is now some recognition in many places that drama is an important if not essential part of the curriculum. This has been a long time coming and has depended on strong and rigorous advocacy from drama educators everywhere. Perhaps now it is time to shift our energies from advocacy to a research rich culture that includes advocacy as one of its aims. This approach builds on the excellent foundations of research in the discipline, but looks to productive collaborations among drama educators to provide further and deeper reasons for the inclusion of drama education in the lives of all students in our schools. This is not an invitation for drama educators and researchers to relax in complacency, but rather for us to provide evidence to those who will continue to question our place in the curriculum.

Teachers as researchers

You will notice that I have made an assumption that if you are reading this chapter, you are interested in researching drama education. I have addressed 'you' throughout the chapter, as 'you' are probably a classroom-based teacher and potential researcher. Where I refer to 'the researcher', I am referring to issues for researchers in education more generally. There are many other sites of drama learning research. Most of the discussion here will address drama learning in classrooms but much of the discussion will be relevant to drama (or applied theatre) in other settings such as hospitals, juvenile justice centres, community groups and so on. I have also dotted examples of studies of drama learning research throughout the chapter to provide examples of how other people have researched the area. This will hopefully inspire you, the beginning researcher.

This chapter is not the last word on educational research. There are plenty of in-depth texts that will give you more detail than I could hope to provide in one chapter. This chapter is designed to demonstrate that drama learning can and should be researched by classroom teachers. The approaches contained in this chapter will hopefully whet your appetite for greater detail that can be found in several books that are devoted solely to doing research (Cohen and Manion, 2000; Freebody, 2003; Denzin and Lincoln, 2005; O' Toole, 2006). The suggested strategies for drama education researchers are for those who would like to deepen their understanding of drama learning by researching their practice and the learning of their students. The chapter will suggest some effective and accessible methodologies for collecting data, discuss ethical issues in this area and suggest some innovative approaches for developing a sustainable culture of reflective practitioner research in this area.

Building theory through research

One of the major challenges for researchers in education is to build theoretical models that allow our research to reach beyond the confines of our classroom or our schools. Theory can be defined as a coherent description and explanation of observed phenomena that can also produce predictions about the behaviour of individuals or groups. Theory is a way that teachers of drama in different contexts can speak about the way that learning occurs. Theory allows researchers to cross borders, boundaries and subjects. Given the usefulness of theory as a way to have rich and deep conversations, you might think it would be a standard fixture in education. The reality according to Kettley, however, is that we are in a state of crisis: '. . . the crisis of theory building in education studies arises from the failure to encourage original interpretations of data among new researchers. Cleaving to existing concepts and isolated paradigms is not imaginative thinking' (2010, p. 9).

The challenge to be imaginative and developing theory is a substantial one for drama educators and a relatively longstanding issue given Gavin Bolton's *Towards a Theory of Drama in Education* appeared in 1979. Since that time the work of Aristotle, Friere, Dewey, Eisner, hooks, Vygotsky, Csikszentmihalyi to name a few, have been enlisted to the cause of theoretical development. Perhaps if we are to take Ketley's call for imaginative thinking further, we might see the emergence of a new batch of theorists from drama education practice. First, however as researchers we need to understand our motivations for undertaking research.

Doing education research

In John O'Toole's (2006) excellent book *Doing Drama Research* he nominates four motives for doing education research:

- To create knowledge for its own sake
- To create knowledge in context
- To create knowledge for a particular context
- To create knowledge in the social context for social reform

As you can see, there are strong research questions that emerge from each of these motives for drama learning. For example, here are some questions could that arise from these motivations:

- How do young people understand and create drama that fights bigotry?
- What drama programs effectively counter bullying?
- Do students who excel in drama improve their oracy and literacy outcomes?
- How do boys learn in drama?

Before we discuss how drama education research might respond to these questions, I would like to contextualize drama within arts education research more broadly.

Arts education research: the context

For perhaps the first time in the history of arts education, there are international and national calls for a renewed examination of the role and benefits of arts education in the lives of young people (Fiske, 1999). In the last decade, there has been a stream of policy, research and advocacy documents that relate to arts and education such as *Champions of Change* (1999) and *Critical Links* (2003) from the Arts Education Partnership and *Evaluation of School-Based Arts Education Programmes in Australian Schools* (2004*).* Internationally UNESCO is developing strategies to support arts education. In its 'Road Map: Aims and Reflections' (UNESCO, 2003), it nominates the following aims for the future of arts education:

- Recognition of Arts Education as a concern of Education
- Consolidation of discussions between the sector of Education and Culture
- Strategies from the governmental organisms to improve the quality of Arts Education
- Designing national and regional policies of research in connection with the specific necessities in the field of Arts Education
- Possibilities to enhance access to Arts Education

Overview of arts education research

There is a growing body of evidence on the positive impact that exposure to the arts can have in the lives of young people. Harland et al. (2000) suggest that art education outcomes range from the most intrinsic, such as enjoyment and personal achievement in the arts themselves, to related effects, such as the development of creativity and divergent thinking, and their extrinsic transfer to other curriculum areas. According to Bower, teaching the arts to students '. . . has been linked to better visual thinking, problem solving, language and creativity . . . by learning and practising art, the human brain actually wires itself to make stronger connections' (2004, p. 23).

While many argue for the richness and complexity of learning in the arts context, arts educators and researchers alike concede that learning in the arts has value beyond the specific art subjects. In *More Than Words Can Say*, Joan Livermore argues that the arts 'can facilitate personal and social development, learning in other curriculum areas and the development of a range of skills and understandings that can be applied in vocational and other life situations' (1998, p. v).

Studies including *Champions of Change* (Fiske, 1999), *Reviewing Education and the Arts Project* (Hetland and Winner, 2001) and *Critical Links* (Deasy, 2002) have indicated that important cognitive and social processes and capabilities are developed in and through arts-learning experiences. As a result, such research has raised awareness of the potential for the arts to enhance learning in the arts themselves, through the arts and across the curriculum and in turn spawned a whole new generation of classroom based researchers.

Arnold Aprill (2001), Executive Director of the Chicago Arts Partnership in Education (CAPE), makes the claim that '... the arts do indeed increase student achievement when achievement is conceived of in rich and complex ways, and when the authentic connections between the arts and the rest of learning are acknowledged and developed over time' (2001, p. 26). However, justifying '... the arts on the basis of their impact on academic performance is not uncontroversial' (p. 180). Those who make this argument are in danger of conceding that other subjects are academically superior, which leads to the undermining of the arts in education.

While much recent research has focused on what Aprill calls 'magic transfer', 'learning in one content area magically generating knowledge or skill in another content area' (2001, p. 26) more often than not, the arts have been the conduit. For example, Floyd (2001) claims that studying music and learning a musical instrument in high school can open the door to a better tertiary education. According to Floyd, students who studied instrumental music averaged up to 304 points higher on their Scholarship Aptitude Tests (SATs). Although such results are encouraging, it is somewhat disappointing that the findings are never reversed. For example, where is the research that argues that the study of grammar makes students better painters, or that learning fractions will result in more effective improvisation or acting skills? Elliot Eisner argues that those seeking information about the positive effects that art has on learning in more traditional academic school subjects should be asked to reverse the question: 'Do reading and maths courses contribute to higher performance in the arts?' (1999, p. 143).

As Eisner consistently argues, 'the arts should be justified in education primarily in relation to their distinctive or unique contributions' (2002, p. 234). Many of the ideas, experiences and learning that occur in the arts are unique to the arts because they are at the centre of cultural expression and understanding (Gibson and Ewing, 2006). Research in arts education has consistently shown that the arts are a distinct form of knowledge requiring sustained and demanding work and yielding kinds of empathy, understanding and skill both equal and distinctive from those available in (other subject disciplines) (Boyer, 2002).

Quality arts education produces positive impacts in terms of 'improved student attitudes to school and learning, enhanced cultural identity and sense of personal satisfaction and well-being' (Bamford, 2006, p. 71). Through arts-based processes, creativity and the imagination can be nurtured since 'the arts are particularly important for experiencing the joy of creating, developing attention to detail, and learning ways of expressing thoughts, knowledge and feelings beyond words' (Upilis and Smithrim, 2003, p. 46).

The research need

The difficulty of working in arts education is that we seem to be forever justifying our existence. We have been arguing for our place in the curriculum through advocating our usefulness and importance to schooling as a whole. Drama education is moving slowly but surely from its beginnings in advocacy-based research to developing an evidence base for its effectiveness in the curriculum. We need researchers with diverse methodological approaches who will allow for a more diverse and deeper series of investigations.

In the remainder of this chapter, I will examine the practicalities of doing research in drama learning. The first step in any research process is to identify what you want to research. In this sense, you are beginning to define your 'inquiry space' or more specifically your research questions. With so much choice the challenge is perhaps to locate a logical achievable question that will sustain the research and not overwhelm you and your available resources.

Finding your research question

Often, potential researchers approach research with a nagging curiosity that manifests itself in the form of a question. The question might be something like: 'What do students get from drama learning?' While on the face of it, this sounds a reasonable question, it betrays a lack of research experience. Without doubt the question is serious, well intentioned and interesting, but it is difficult to manage as research since the question is too vague and too broad. There are several 100,000-word dissertations on this one little question alone. This question contains myriad sub-questions. While it is necessary to have sub-questions, they should not be of such a multitude that they overwhelm the initial question.

When you are developing a research question, it is worth remembering that the questions you arrive at have involved you in a process of choice. One way to formalize these choices is to set out in a three-column table the different questions you are considering. In the first column, write all the questions you are considering. In the second, write all the sub-questions that emerge from the questions, and in the third, record some of the methodologies and strategies you think might be useful to examine your questions. The final stage of this process is analysing which of your questions is the most 'researchable' – which of the questions can be undertaken feasibly by you within the resources you have available to you.

In research, you choose to open doors to some questions and close the door on others. These closed doors represent other opportunities, other research questions to be pursued later. It is better to put these opportunities on hold rather than bloat your initial question to the point where the research cannot be managed. When you do make these choices, it is important to acknowledge the limitations of your research in the publications that emerge. Acknowledging research limitations indicates to those reviewing or examining your research that you know that you have made logical and deliberate choices about the range and the scope of your research.

Refining the research question

To begin, you need a question that will 'sit in the palm of your hand' – it will be self-contained and self-explanatory. The question should be specific enough so that the way you examine the question seems logical. Instead of asking 'what do students get from drama learning?' You might ask: 'Do students have improved literacy outcomes after undertaking drama learning?' or 'Do students become more critically literate when they undertake drama learning?' or 'Does drama learning create social cohesion in the classroom?' The following Table 9.1 outlines these questions, some of the sub-questions that arise and suggests some of the research strategies that could be used to explore these areas.

Table 9.1 Organizing the research question

Research question	Research sub-questions	Research methodology and strategies
Do student have improved literacy scores after undertaking drama?	• Does drama learning effect student's literacy differently at different ages/ stages of schooling? • What kind of literacy does it improve? (Oracy, reading, writing etc.)	• Collect student literacy scores from tests in the targeted class • Teach an intensive drama course with these students (intervention) • Test students after the course and compare the results with other students who have not undertaken drama intervention
Do students become more critically literate when they undertake drama?	• Does drama help students critically analyse social situations (gender roles, status etc.)? • Does drama help students critically analyse other art forms (novels etc.)? • Do the skills of critical literacy transfer into other areas of learning?	• Ask students to analyse a piece of drama before learning skills for critical literacy • Provide students with critical literacy skills that relate to the analysis of the drama • Ask students to analyse a different piece of drama and record the difference in language used and its application to the analysis process
Does drama learning create social cohesion in the classroom?	• What elements of drama (if any) create social cohesion? • Does drama learning create social cohesion for students from disadvantaged backgrounds? • Does this social cohesion manifest in other areas of schooling?	• Interview students prior to being involved in a drama project about teamwork and collaboration • Undertake a playbuilding project with these students. As this project progresses ask them to keep a journal or a blog that relates to team work and team building • Interview the students after the project specifically asking them about their learning about teamwork and collaboration

This table is not intended to provide in-depth methodological responses to questions. Rather it makes the point that methodology is often inherent within the question. The questions should be specific enough to support a clear, well defined and deliberate examination of a 'research problem'. As you delve deeper into your inquiry space, the evidence may lead you to change the question in some way. Changing the question is usually part of the research process. The researcher must be allowed to alter the course slightly as long as the integrity of the area is maintained. When you have decided on the question and sub-questions, the next step is to read around the areas that you are interested in with the ultimate aim of constructing a literature review. The literature review will help to refine and perhaps will even change your research question.

Managing the written reflection: first steps

As a beginning researcher, your written research reflection (thesis, dissertation etc.) may only be 10,000 to 20,000 words. This may seem like a great many words, but once the structural parts of the written research reflection (literature review, methodology, conclusions etc.) are accounted for, there is not much space left for the discussion of a broad topic.

A good starting point when you have settled on a question is to find a thesis of the same length (which may or may not be related to your question) and read it. This will give you a feel for the length of the work and what length each of your chapters might be. The next step is to plan out your chapters and allocate a 'word budget' to them. A word budget indicates how long you think each area might be. For instance, you might decide that the literature review is to be 5000 words. The effect of this is that in a 20,000-word thesis, you have 15,000 words remaining. It also allows you to keep track of where you have over-written.

Finding the literature

The literature search/review should express the supporting evidence for the research question and the gap in the literature that the research question is addressing. If you discover during the literature search that the specifics of your question have been addressed, you might need to recast the question so that your approach is addressing a gap in the literature. The question must be original in the sense that your specific question has not been asked in this way. Thankfully, technology has made finding and collecting relevant literature much more manageable.

Research focused web-based search engines such as Google scholar, A+ Education and Endnote have radically changed the process of a literature search. Ten years ago, researchers might have sat isolated in a library poring over journals and edited books for citations that they would then pursue through journals, taking weeks and often months to get what they needed. Today researchers associated with universities have virtually instantaneous access to research materials that can be brought directly to their desktop and used as part of their literature review. Apart from the obvious saving in time, this approach also allows researchers to see further than their own disciplines and survey the literature from other fields. For instance, in drama learning, the disciplines of education, cultural studies, aesthetics, performance studies, organizational psychology and so on may be relevant to a research question. While researchers might know their own field in depth, it is unlikely that they would know these other areas in the same detail. These search technologies provide massive amounts of irrelevance, but they also uncover valuable areas of research in sometimes quite unrelated areas. For example, drama educators have recently made connection with researchers making video games for learning (Carroll et al., 2006). In both drama education and video games research, protocols that relate to role and simulation have been the subject of research attention. This has led to some exciting opportunities for researchers in both areas to collaborate and examine real-life questions that are not restricted to disciplinary borders. In the twenty-first century, the convergence of technologies and disciplines will require researchers to skip nimbly between their home discipline and other areas of research. Existing and emerging technologies make this possible.

Crafting your literature view

The craft of literature review is to identify the research and scholarship that is most pertinent to your research question. This process is like a set of radiating circles (see Figure 9.1).

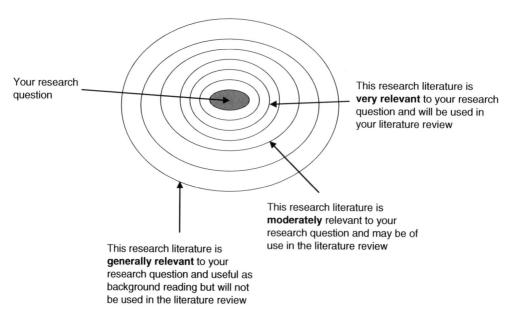

Figure 9.1 The radiating circles of research literature relevance

At the centre of the circle is the research question. As this question addresses a gap in the research literature, there should be nothing that covers exactly the same ground as your question. For instance, your question might be 'does drama learning provide students from inner-city Newcastle with creative skills that can assist them to find work when they leave school?' While there will be no specific studies on this, because this is your focus question, there will be studies that relate to students from inner-city areas finding work after leaving school. There will also be studies on the link between schooling and work and so on. The radiating circles relate to the relevance of the research literature as it addresses your research question. As your literature review continues, you will find literature that supports the basis of your research and other research that might represent the outer circles that are not as relevant. The research on the outer circles may be useful to file as background, but probably will not become a central part of your research question. When you have arrived at a question, you will then need to determine which research methodology will serve the needs of your question.

Finding methodology: rejecting false dichotomies

There has been a strong and useful argument in education about how we should examine research questions. Habitually arguments have usually fallen into a dichotomy: the qualitative versus the quantitative. As Carroll argues (1996, p. 74), we should be mindful that all methodologies are human constructions and have inherent political, historical and gender bias. Having accepted that objectivity is a myth, we can then discuss the more important question: what methodology will suit the needs of the question? In some cases, it will suit the research question to run a quantitative analysis; in other cases a more complex design will be necessary. Sometimes both will be required to adequately explore an issue. The approaches discussed here might be implemented over a series of lessons as a short-term or cross-sectional study that allows researchers to examine many cases over a short period of time. Other research projects may take a number of years in a longitudinal study. Longitudinal studies examine '. . . features of people or other units at more than one time' (Newman, 2006). The longitudinal design is relevant to arts learning as it allows examination of the possibility and significance of change (or no change) over time. Time allows consequences to take place. The length of the study usually corresponds to the nature of the question, the available resources and the space available to report the outcomes of the question.

Quantitative research: findings with 'hard edges'

In drama learning, quantitative methodology does have its place. It can give an overall summary of simple information such as: 'How many students study drama in school?' or 'Does drama learning improve literacy scores?' When delving into the complexities of the learning experience, qualitative methodology is a natural choice. As Elliot Eisner (1978, p. 201) points out in exploring the complexities of educational research, there is little to be gained in reducing the '. . . human mind to a single score'. Conversely, the qualitative method attempts to '. . . adumbrate its complexities, its potential, and its idiosyncrasies' (1978, p. 201).

Within the double speak that sometimes passes for discussion in bureaucracies, there are often calls for findings with 'hard edges'. What perhaps this means is findings that can show significance in a statistical way. For instance:

> X% of students achieve higher numeracy scores as a result of drama learning.

There is of course an inbuilt discrimination in a call for 'hard edged data' as it presupposes that anything important can be demonstrated in a quantitative way. Most educators agree that the complexity of classroom learning is difficult to reflect with quantitative methodologies. The collaboration and interactions of drama learning make this interaction potentially more complex. Our praxis is so heavily based in experience, intuition and human interactions that much of our research depends on understanding and interpreting the lived classroom experiences of students and teachers. This kind of research does not always come with hard edges. We should continue to qualitatively examine and report the depth of what goes on in learning and particularly drama learning by searching for new methodologies that represent the complexity of learning in drama. Whichever methodology you choose, be aware of the audience we are attempting to persuade. If our aim is to advocate our case to policymakers, perhaps we will need to speak the language of quantitative research to make our point. If we are striving to describe the complexities inherent in drama learning, we could continue using existing and new methodologies where they suit our research question and are able to describe the multidimensional nature of drama learning. Many questions that teachers are exploring in the classroom are too complex to be examined through quantitative methods alone.

Marianne Mansour did her initial teacher education training in drama. Her Doctoral research is investigating the potential advantages of arts education on students' motivation, engagement, and achievement. With the present surge in advocacy involving the arts and education (Gibson and Anderson, 2008), this research will ascertain an evidence base which focuses on the academic benefits of in-school and out-of-school arts-related programs. How does arts education participation impact academic motivation, engagement, and achievement? The research approach and questions are currently being tested using quantitative methods among a large sample of primary and secondary school students. Data is being collected in 2010 and again, in 2011. Longitudinal analyses comprising the same measures one year later enable structural models to establish the causal ordering of the role of arts education on academic (and non-academic) factors. This kind of quantitative analysis will inform the next part of this process. The qualitative phase being handled by another drama educator. Caitlin Munday will use the outcomes of the quantitative phase to identify high quality arts learning environments. These learning environments will be analysed to assist in describing the features of high quality learning in drama and other arts classrooms.

Qualitative research

Qualitative research has had a 'distinguished place in the human disciplines' since the 1920s and 1930s (Denzin and Lincoln, 1994, p. 1). The growth and development of qualitative research paralleled the need for a more powerful and naturalistic research method than positivism (Eisner, 1978, p. 202). Bruner (1990, p. 130) says: '. . . neither the empiricist's tested knowledge nor the rationalist's self-evident truths describe the ground on which ordinary people go about making sense of their experiences'. Qualitative research allows researchers to delve into the layered complexity of lived human experience. Research into drama learning requires methodology that allows for the complexity and idiosyncrasies that are inherent in a process of group creativity. The depth of analysis possible in qualitative research is not available in more reductionist methodologies. As Grady (1996) argues, to deal with the complexity of human experience, research should be undertaken from an informed position, which allows the researcher to '. . . choose challenging rhetorical and methodological tools that allow us to focus on the complexities of the practice of theory in practice' (Grady, 1996, p. 70).

Eisner defines qualitative methodology as: '. . . that form of inquiry that seeks the creation of qualities that are expressively patterned, that seeks the explication of wholes as the primary aim, that emphasizes the study of configurations rather than isolated entities, that regards expressive narratives and visuals as appropriate vehicles for communication' (1978, p. 198). This definition identifies several key elements of drama learning. His identification of the 'creation of qualities that are expressively patterned' (1978, p. 198) reflects the central significance of identifying the quality of the learning experience through its features. Even though drama learning is context specific, the research findings from one place will have resonances to other teachers in other places. This approach seeks to analyse each specific context to create broader understanding of the drama learning experience of teachers and students. Denzin and Lincoln (2005, p. 3) also argue this kind of research has the power to transform because it has immediate relevance to its community, in our case the drama classroom. They argue that qualitative research is '. . . a situated activity that locates the observer in the world . . . qualitative research involves an interpretative, naturalistic approach to the world. This means that qualitative researchers study things in their natural settings, attempting to make sense of, or to interpret, phenomena in terms of the meanings people bring to them' (2005, p. 3). Qualitative approaches fit well with research that seeks to transform learning rather than just depict or reflect current practice.

Mixed methods approaches

Mixed methods approach can examine a large set of questions in the middle ground between qualitative and quantitative methods (Johnson and Onwuegbuzie, 2004, p. 15). They argue mixed method research occurs: '. . . where the researcher mixes or combines quantitative and qualitative research techniques, methods, approaches, concepts or language into a single study. Philosophically, it is the "third wave" or third research movement, a movement that moves past the paradigm wars by offering a logical and practical alternative' (p. 17). For example, this approach could allow a researcher to use a survey to examine why certain groups of students do not engage with drama learning. The results of this survey may lead to conclusions that suggest further analysis. In the analysis of these survey results, you might undertake a cluster analysis that groups variables. Maybe your variables are student access to technology, student literacy scores and engagement in drama learning. For instance, the survey found a group of students with low literacy scores and high access technology did not engage with drama learning. This is a potentially very interesting finding. The problem is, however, the quantitative analysis tells us that the relationship exists but does not tell us why. To examine why, the researcher would need to use a qualitative approach such as interview or case study of those within this group. This approach has the potential to provide the quantitative measurement that policymakers crave and the qualitative responses that many educators require to explain the complexity of learning in the classroom. Johnson and Onwuegbuzie (2004) argue that this method has the potential to unify elements of educational research and examine research questions that cannot be examined by qualitative or quantitative research alone. 'By narrowing the divide between quantitative and qualitative researchers, mixed methods research has a great potential to promote a shared responsibility in the quest for attaining accountability for educational quality' (2004, p. 24). There are however some questions that are suited to qualitative methods alone. We will spend the remainder of the chapter exploring methods that are relevant to drama learning in the classroom.

Research approaches that examine details: ethnomethodology

Ethnomethodology is a social research methodology that explores the relationships between '. . . social order, the observable regularities of social activities, and the role of social members in the production of those regularities' (Freebody and Freiberg, 2011, p. 79) and as such have wide application for settings like classrooms. Ethnomethodological techniques in the drama classroom allow for a more fine-grained and detailed view of learning in individual classrooms. Perhaps more importantly, they provide researchers with an understanding of the experience of being in a drama classroom, known to ethnomethodologists as the 'haecceity' or the 'thisness' of the classroom research setting. Anyone who has spent time in a drama classroom will be able to tell you of the detail that creates learning and meaning for participants. It is this attention to the sometimes-overlooked detail of drama learning that may be behind the power of ethnomethodological techniques in the classroom. These techniques can provide insights into learning that have been overlooked in the rush to provide evidence of the power of learning in drama classrooms (which has sometimes has been used to fuel advocacy discussions with educational gatekeepers). The advent of methodologies in drama education research examining detailed interactions is a welcome addition to the field.

Kelly Freebody (2010) used drama pedagogy to explore students' interpretations of, and interaction with, notions of Socio-Economic Status (SES). Her work analysed the way talk categorizes young people in drama. Her findings suggest that this methodology can present researchers with fine-grained understandings of the ways young people interact in the drama classroom to define their social understandings about themselves and others. Her study examined two classes in schools with contrasting SES settings. The teachers were provided with lesson plans detailing a process drama called *The Future* that asked students to invent, explore and enact possible scenarios concerning their perceptions of their own future pathways. The lessons were recorded and transcribed, with Conversation Analysis (CA) and Member Categorization Analysis (MCA) that are used to understand the particular ways the students oriented to implicit or explicit shared understandings of cultural categories associated with social and economic structures. The study found that during the lessons, the students and teachers engaged in three types of talk-in-interaction:

- talk that managed school and lesson behaviour – termed Pedagogic/Logistic Talk (PLT);
- talk that engaged participants in the cultural, social and moral potential of the lesson and aimed to create shared accounts and public reasoning practices – termed Socio-Cultural Talk (SCT); and
- talk that took place when students were in role, which allowed students to demonstrate their understandings of the expectations signalled in the SCT and to improvise reactions to scenarios in role as character-participants in a drama – termed In Role Talk (IRT).

Ethnomethodological researchers have demonstrated the utility of this kind of approach in real-world settings where classroom interactions are complex. In her research, Kelly Freebody (2010) suggests that ethnomethodological research techniques are suited to research in these learning environments:

> Drama and CA/MCA provided the researcher with naturally occurring data, in an environment where participants had opportunities to explore social issues from numerous levels, including the embodiment of particular discourses (e.g., about SES, parenthood, responsibility) and the 'acting out' of shared understandings negotiated through earlier classroom discussion. That data was then analysed rigorously through the use of CA/MCA to investigate ways in which participants interact with each other, itself providing a context to explore discourses relating to SES in Australia, as understood and oriented to by the members of a particular group. (2008, pp. 257–8)

While ethnomethodological techniques can deal effectively with spoken interactions, it is the complex interactions between the body and the mind that may go unresearched by using this method exclusively. This is an inevitable consequence of classroom research with almost any method where some interactions are selected while others remain uncaptured. CA/MCA focusses on specific aspects of the classroom interaction (namely talk and membership categories) and has limited capacity to track and analyse the complexities of the mind/body interaction. This feature of the methodology will limit its scope to capture the macro features of the pedagogy in classrooms that have a large embodied learning component. On the other hand, there is much that could be learnt from research that uses CA/MCA in concert with other techniques to cover the classroom terrain. Developing a multi-method approach where ethnomethodological approaches (CA/MCA especially) are employed to reflect the part and the whole of classroom, interactions may allow us to analyse classroom interactions at a particular and holistic level simultaneously.

For teachers, ethnomethodology has the capacity to uncover the detail of teaching. Perhaps in this granularity, educators might glimpse some of the entrenched deep rationalities that hinder educational change. For researchers, there are exciting prospects for this approach to be used with other research strategies to tell a broad and deep story about learning and the potential for change in classrooms.

Case study

A case study is defined as '. . . the study of the particularity of and complexity of a single case, coming to understand its activity within important circumstances' (Stake, 1995). Exploring teachers' experience of teaching drama or students learning in the subject provides a rich, deep and complex picture to analyse. Although generalizations cannot be made as a result of that analysis, it is an insight into a process at a – to use a filmmaking analogy – 'close-up' context of the teacher in the classroom and the 'mid-shot' context of teacher and their school, that may illuminate the 'wide-shot' concerns of drama teaching in the context of the curriculum. 'They [the research participants] may be similar or dissimilar, redundancy and variety each having voice. They are chosen because it is believed that understanding them will lead to a better understanding perhaps better theorizing, about a still larger set of cases' (Stake, 2000, p. 437).

Participants in drama research are specific and unique 'cases' who have their own constructed realities. Having several 'cases' affords the researcher the opportunity of making comparisons and contrasts that may lead to a better understanding of the wider world of drama learning and learning more generally. The information drawn for comment from these cases will obviously reflect the research question or as Stake argues: 'My choice would be to take from the case from which we feel we can learn the most' (1994, p. 243). Consequently when material is chosen from the interview transcripts and developed into narratives, material should be selected that is most appropriate to the themes and sub-themes of the research.

Interviews

Interviews provide a way to discover the attitudes, recollections and understandings about a certain research topic in some depth. The aim of this strategy is to engage in a conversation that creates mutually constructed meaning. The most useful research interview in my view is the semi-structured interview. In the semi-structured interview, the participant and the researcher both have input into the process. This type of interview is more honest, morally sound and reliable as it treats the respondent as an equal, allows them to express personal feelings and therefore presents a more 'realistic' picture than can be uncovered using traditional methods. As Fontana and Frey (1994, p. 373) argue: 'Forgetting the rules [of traditional interviewing] . . . allows research subjects to express themselves more freely, and thus to have greater voice both in research process and in the research report' (1994, p. 368).

Often these types of interviews begin with a discussion about the process that encourages the participants to negotiate the interview as it progresses. The participants have the right not to answer questions, ask questions of the researcher and add their own observations of the process. At any stage they can terminate the interview. Video can be used to record the interview that captures the non-verbal features of the discussion (Fontana and Frey, 1994, p. 371) that may be important in the data analysis process.

There are still problems with this more informal style of interviewing. This approach supports the idea of a discussion although the interviewer's first task is to listen. As Ely comments (1991, p. 67): 'LISTEN, LISTEN and LISTEN MORE.' Even though there is a collaborative element, the first priority is to listen to the story. To do otherwise is to reinstate the hierarchy of the researcher espousing wisdom and the 'researched' responding. Researchers have to resist the temptation to add their own commentary on the situation they are researching. The conversational style of this interaction facilitates this kind of response. The research methodology, however, is attempting to reflect the participant's experiences and not the interventions of the researcher.

Participatory action research

Participatory action research comes closest to the ideal of praxis: practice and action as research. Participatory action research '. . . typically involves the use of qualitative interpretative modes of inquiry and data collection by teachers (often with the help of academics) with a view to teachers making judgements about how to improve their own practice . . . . The emphasis is "practical", that is on the interpretations that teachers and students are making and acting on in the situation' (Kemmis and McTaggart, 2005, p. 561). The focus for participatory action researchers is on improving the situations in which they work, be it a classroom, a hospital or a business. There has been some criticism that this method founded on the progressivism of the 1970s and 1980s has fallen short of its ambitious aims of changing the world. In response to this criticism, Kemmis argues that participatory action researchers '. . . may not have changed the world but they have changed their worlds' (Kemmis and McTaggart, 2005, p. 600). This research method is suited to arts classrooms as it allows those engaged in drama learning to change their worlds in the absence of organized systemic support and to enrich their own practice by researching it.

In participatory action research, teachers devise a research question that relates directly to their practice such as 'how can I teach playbuilding skills to a group of Year 9 students using the principles inherent in productive pedagogies'. The teacher would then (perhaps with the assistance of another researcher) design an intervention (a group of lessons on characterization) and then put it into action (teach the lessons). As the lessons take place, data is collected perhaps through interviews, participant logbooks or observation to reflect what is going on in the intervention. The concluding reflection provides an in-depth examination of the learning process that may then be linked to advances in theoretical discussions that relate to learning.

Ethical considerations

No discussion of research can or should omit the ethical challenges that face researchers. In education, we are faced with some especially challenging ethical dilemmas as our research participants are often young children. If we are serious about researching our own classroom practice, we must accept that there are some ethical questions to be reconciled and resolved during research. If you are undertaking research within a school that involves students or teachers, you will need to obtain ethical clearances. This has a twin purpose. It lets your system (university, school etc.) know what you are doing and allows others to peer review the ethical robustness of your planned research. While there are whole books devoted to the ethics of research in education, this section will deal with those issues that I think are pertinent to drama learning: anonymity and confidentiality, transparency and informed consent.

Anonymity and confidentiality

Researchers take different views about anonymity in educational research. Punch argues, '. . . there is strong feeling among most fieldworkers that settings and respondents should not be identifiable in print, and that they should not suffer harm or embarrassment as a consequence of research' (1994, p. 93). Other researchers such as Shulman (1990, p. 11) take a very different view claiming that participants' voices should be recognized. However, she also points to the consequences and implications of revealing participant identities that may single them out for ridicule and oppression. Her study into the attitudes of teachers in classrooms left her participants potentially vulnerable as '. . . teachers rarely leave the scene [of research]. They must bear the burden of their written words, for they remain participants long after they complete their roles . . .' (Shulman, 1990, p. 14).

Anonymity often empowers research participants to speak out about their experience of other teachers, colleagues or supervisors in ways that would be impossible if they were identified publicly (Shulman, 1990, p. 11). Pseudonyms are useful for the research participants, participants' schools and any other person who could be identified or identify others. Broad geographical areas can be used to identify and contextualize the location of the research participants. My advice is to take the safe course and make your participants anonymous. Your participants may decide that they would like to associate themselves with the research, but that should be left to them.

Transparency: informed consent

In research that seeks to include participants as partners, informed consent is crucial. It provides a transparency for the motives of the research that cannot be assured if there is deception in the research process. For instance, if you are exploring if drama learning promotes participation in democratic processes, the following description could appear in your participant information sheet:

> This study will explore whether drama learning encourages participation in democratic processes. In this study, we will interview you about your participation in politics and your interest with democratic processes such as voting. At no time during this process will you be asked to reveal your political views.

This clearly and in plain English outlines the intent of the study and the expectation of the participants. It also lets the research participants know what they will not be asked to reveal. I cannot think of a reason that participants in drama learning research (or any kind of educational research) should be deceived. This approach keeps faith with those we are working with and addresses the inherent imbalance between the researcher and the researched. As many of the qualitative approaches we suggest here are not generalizable, we need to search for alternative approaches to validity, reliability and credibility.

Seeking validity, reliability and credibility

Validity reflects the extent to which your research is '. . . sound, cogent, well grounded, justifiable or logically correct' (Schwandt, 2001). If research is credible, it should be trustworthy (Schwandt, 2001) in that it truly reflects the authentic voice of the participants and resonates with others who will be engaged by the research. Many qualitative methodologies seek to remove the traditional researcher and researched status. This partnership can be maintained by ensuring that the research participants feel that the research undertaken with them reflects what they feel they wanted to communicate as part of the research. Giving research participants an opportunity to respond to their contribution ensures the reliability and the credibility of the research. Research participants may ask for changes to the research; even though the researcher may disagree with these sentiments, they have the right to be represented in ways that they feel are valid. Naturally, this requires negotiation on the part of the researcher and the participants, but the voice and wishes of the participants are central to the validity of the research. The credibility of the research lies in the authenticity and clarity of the research participants' voices and their transferability, creating knowledge that leads to a deeper understanding of the research question.

Crystallization

There are some useful measures of credibility here, but in my experience one of the most useful is crystallization. Along with the authenticity of research participants' voice this is an important part of the developing reliability of qualitative research. Triangulation is a well known method that employs a variety of data sources in a study (Janesick, 1994, p. 214). It is a useful term but does suggest limitation. I prefer the crystallization method as it has greater scope to validate the data. Laurel Richardson (1994) says the '. . . central image for "validity" for postmodernist texts is not the triangle – a rigid, fixed, two-dimensional object. Rather, the central image is the crystal, which combines symmetry and substance with an infinite variety of shapes, substances, transmutations, multidimensionalities, and angles of approach. Crystals grow change, alter but are not amorphous' (1994, p. 522).

Crystallization seems more able to describe several approaches to validating the research data. The process also reflects the possibility of several reflections from the same source, in other words several interpretations from the one interview, narrative or case study. The researcher's interpretations may be only one of the many interpretations possible. For instance, if your study examined teachers' experience of the classroom through narratives, you might use several methods of validation for the narratives. First, the teachers in the study could validate the narratives (one facet of the crystal) by reading and responding to the narratives indicating whether they are a valid reflection of their experience. At any point, they could negotiate changes and make additions to the narratives. This validation allows the authentic voices of participants to emerge and ensures the researcher's style or voice does not overwhelm the participants' voices. Another facet of this crystallization process might be meant to bring in other researchers to analyse interviews, narratives and case studies and suggest other interpretations of the data.

Conclusions

We have reached a moment in the history of drama education like no other before. For the first time in living memory, there are international and national calls for a renewed examination of the role of arts education in the lives of young people. Discussions are occurring with policy makers about the place of education and UNESCO is taking notice of the power that arts education provides. There are now several documents outlining the areas where research might be undertaken and there is a new generation of drama education scholars gaining their metaphorical wings.

The time is right for drama researchers to examine our strong research heritage and plan for the future in partnership with other drama and arts educators in schools or hospitals or youth outreach centres throughout the country and the world. We now have the potential to influence policy makers and make the arts a priority in the learning of every young person through a sustained, creative and relevant drama education research culture. We may not have this chance again in our lifetimes.

Note

1 I am aware that in many places, advocacy is still required to get drama into the curriculum. There is a place for this research, but in my view it needs to be balanced with research that works on supporting and analysing our current and future practice to ensure drama education continues to be dynamic.

Epilogue: Teaching critical hope through drama

So what could our response be, what might we do to sustain drama education and cultivate it for this and the next generation of learners? How might we convince the gatekeepers: the bureaucrats, the bankers, business people and politicians, those who whether we like it or not will make decisions about the future of education, that drama has a unique and crucial place in learning. I would like to outline three principles that I think will make a contribution to developing the argument for drama as a pedagogy suited to the needs of generation next.

Developing critical hope

Paulo Friere (2004, p. 2) argued that 'we need critical hope the way a fish needs unpolluted water'. As I ponder what might be next for drama education, I marvel at the changes that have already happened in my lifetime and I look forward to the changes that must now come, urgently. In the midst of all this change, there are two foundations drama learning is anchored to. The first foundation is the aesthetics of drama and theatre. Our art form is robust and dynamic and even though critics have been pronouncing theatre dead for decades, it still remains, resolutely prominent in our society and our schools. Perhaps more crucial is the second foundation; the power of drama for learning. Drama education offers young people access to critical hope where they can appraise the world and learn to be participants in the world as it changes, not as passengers but as drivers. Critical hope does not teach passivity; it develops informed optimism that helps students to understand the world through their minds, bodies and emotions. If through drama we can provide the capacity for critical hope, it will be perhaps the most significant contribution we can make to an active, engaged and critical society.

Equipping the field for the challenges of the twenty-first century

The challenges for twenty-first century learning go far beyond the interaction of technology and education. There are real and pressing social issues around tolerance, citizenship and engagement with the politics of the environment. The list goes on and on. Perhaps the new questions are no different from the old, but they do feel more pressing and more imminent as the world looks on as politicians lack the courage to move on climate change and other issues in the face of powerful vested interests. As people who care about sustaining a peaceful, democratic society, we need to develop drama teaching that equips young people to be the designers of their own destiny. If we are to meet these challenges, we need to get going now. We need leaders who 'get' schools, who understand research and above all who understand that for drama education to grow and prosper. We need to grapple with the looming issues and support drama educators working in schools, theatre companies, community groups or wherever they are to face these issues. Head on, courageously, authentically and truthfully.

And that's in a sense my third point . . . authenticity and truth. Beyond all of the discussions about politics and research strategy and approach, the reason I am still a drama educator is the moment that I glimpsed in Ryan (who I introduced to you at the beginning of this book). Way back in that mid-1980s classroom. While it is a much reported narrative and not necessarily one that will get funding or cut much ice with bureacrats, it is the reason I still teach drama. It is the power of drama to tell the truth through a lie that continues to astound and inspire me. To find the authentic in artifice, to be critically hopeful.

Drama educators need to teach truth telling

I know in a world which is full of relativisms, the 'truth' is not a particularly palatable concept. But artists, be they dancers, sculptors, actors, directors, or musicians, spend most of their lives searching for ways to communicate the truth of the human existence. The artist Allan Moore says that 'Artists use lies to tell the truth'. And of course he is right. The fictions that we create in drama for instance are really only effective when there is something authentic, something we can relate to, something true about what we are performing. One of my favourite playwrights Tom Stoppard examined this in *The Real Thing* written in 1982. The main character Henry is having an arguement about good art and truth with his partner Annie. She is about to star in a dreadful melodramatic play, and he says of the play and art in general . . . .

> What we're trying to do is write cricket bats, so that when we throw up an **idea** and give it a little knock, it might . . . travel . . . ([He] picks up the script.) Now, what we've got here is a lump of wood of roughly the same shape trying to be a cricket bat, and if you hit a ball with it, the ball would travel about ten feet and you will drop the bat and dance about shouting 'Ouch!' with your hands stuck into your armpits (indicating the cricket bat). This isn't better because someone says it's better, or because there's a conspiracy by the MCC to keep cudgels out of Lords. It's better because it's better. (1982)

Henry's point is that crafting a great piece of art that speaks truth is not easy, but it is worth the effort. It is worth seeking out the truth and creating great art to communicate that truth to others. This of course takes, time, effort, skill and above all courage, but it is central to what drama learning is all about. That is why drama education is vital, not because it helps us do sums better or get on better with our workmates (although those things are important) but because it allows us to craft lies that tell the truth about ourselves and about our community. It speaks a truth that some will not enjoy hearing but it is truth all the same.

As we seek to develop our field and extend the boundaries of our research and teaching to meet the needs of a new generation, I would encourage all of us to think of searching for truth and authenticity. I hope our future discussions around drama pedagogy prepares us for the challenges that lie ahead but for me, more importantly I hope that it reminds us at the centre of the critical hope that we strive for is a student, perhaps a student like Ryan who is oblivious to research politics, oblivious to gatekeepers, oblivious to curriculum politics. Our responsibility to the Ryans of this world is through truthful and authentic pedagogies, research and community engagement to create critical hope that will help him and young people like him to rewrite the world.

References

Abbs, P. (2003). *Against the Flow: Education, the Arts and Postmodern Culture*. London: Routledge Falmer.

Ackroyd, J. (1999). Applied theatre: Problems and possibilities. *Applied Theatre Researcher* [Online serial]. Available www.gu.edu/centre/atr

Aitken, V. (2009). Conversations with status and power: how Everyday Theatre offers 'spaces of agency' to participants. *Research in Drama Education: The Journal of Applied Theatre and Performance,* 14(4), 503–27.

Alfred, G. Byram, M. and Fleming, M. (2003). Introduction. In G. Alfred, M. Byram and M. Fleming (eds), *Intercultural Experience and Education* (pp. 1–14). Clevedon: Multilingual Matters.

Anderson, M. (2002). *Journeys in Teacher Professional Development.* Unpublished doctoral thesis, University of Sydney.

— (2004). Devising unities: A recent history of drama education in NSW. In *The State of Our Art. NSW Perspectives in Drama Education.* Strawberry Hills, NSW: Currency Press, pp. 3–18.

Anderson, M. and Jefferson, M. (2009). *Teaching the Screen: Film Education for Generation Next* Crows Nest, NSW: Allen and Unwin.

Anon (1986). Farewell to 'the Mole': A brief tribute to Dorothy Heathcote. *2D,* 6, p. 81.

Apple, M. (1991). The new technology: Is it part of the solution or part of the problem? *Computers in the Schools,* 8 59–81.

Aprill, A. (2001). Toward a finer description of the connection between arts education and student achievement. *Arts Education Policy Review,* 102(5), pp. 25–6.

Arnold, R. (1994). Drama Psychodynamics and english education. *English in Australia, Journal of the Association for the Teaching of English,* 10, 17–27.

Arnold, R. and Hughes, J. (2005). *The Importance of Inter/Intra Subjectivity in Students' Perceptions of Teacher Effectiveness: An Empathically Intelligent Approach to Understanding.* Parramatta, Sydney: International Education Research Conference.

Australia Council for Education Research (ACER). (2004). *Evaluation of School-Based Arts Education Programmes in Australian Schools.* Canberra, ACT: ACER.

Australian Curriculum, Assessment and Reporting Authority (2010). *Shape of the* Australian *Curriculum: The Arts,* Retrieved 10 November 2010, from www.acara.edu.au/verve/_resources/Draft+Shape+Of+The+Australian+Curriculum+The+Arts-FINAL.pdf

Bamford, A. (2006). *The WOW Factor: Global Research Compendium on the Impact of Arts in Education.* New York: Waxmann Munster.

Barab, S. A., Barnett, M. G. and Squire, K. (2002). Developing an empirical account of a community of practice: Characterizing the essential tensions. *The Journal of the Learning Sciences,* 11(4), 489–542.

Barker, H. (1997). *Arguments for a Theatre.* Manchester, UK: University Press.

Baroski, K. (2009). Voices from the ghetto: Youth drama from Houston's at-risk youth. *Contemporary Learning Center,* 34–52.

Bennett, S., Maton, K. and Kervin, L. (2008). The 'digital natives' debate: A critical review of the evidence. *British Journal of Educational Technology,* 39(5), 775–86.

Black, P. and William, D. (1998). Assessment and classroom learning. *Assessment in Education,* 5(1), 7–74.

— (2004). Classroom assessment is not (necessarily) formative assessment (and vice-versa). In M. Wilson (ed.), *Towards Coherence Between Classroom Assessment and Accountability: 103rd Yearbook of the National Society for the Study of Education* (pp. 183–8). Chicago: University of Chicago Press.

Boal, A. (2000). *Theatre of the Oppressed*, 3rd edn. London: Pluto Press.

Bolton, G. (1980). Theatre form in Drama Teaching. In K. Robinson (ed.), *Exploring Theatre and Education* (pp. 71–87). London: Heineman.

— (1986). *Gavin Bolton: Selected Writings on Drama in Education*. London: Longman.

— (1998). *Acting in Classroom Drama: A Critical Analysis*. Oakhill, TX: Trentham Books.

Bowell, P and Heap, B. (2002). *Planning Process Drama*. London: David Fulton.

Bower, S. (2004). Developing a yearning for primary learning: A focus on literature and the creative and practical arts. *Australian Art Education*, 7(2), 21–8.

Boyer, E. (2002). *Becoming Knowledge: The Evolution of Art Education Curriculum*. Retrieved 31 December 2006, from www.newhorizons.org

British Broadcasting Corporation. (1976). *Three Looms Waiting*. London: British Broadcasting Corporation.

Brook, P. (1968). *The Empty Space*. London: MacGibbon and Kee.

Bruner, J. (1977). *The Process of Education*. Cambridge: Harvard University Press.

— (1990). *Acts of Meaning*. Cambridge: Harvard University Press.

Buckingham, D. (2008). Introducing identity. In D. Buckingham (ed.), *Youth, Identity, and Digital Media* (pp. 1–24). The John D. and Catherine T. MacArthur Foundation Series on Digital Media and Learning. Cambridge, MA: MIT Press.

Carey, J. (2006). *What Good Are the Arts?* New York: Oxford University Press.

Carroll, J., Howard, S., Peck, J. and Murphy (2002). A field study of perceptions and use of mobile telephones by 16 to 22 year olds. *Journal of Information Technology Theory and Application*, 4(2), 49–62.

Carrol, J., Anderson, M. and Cameron, D. (2006). *Real players? Drama, Technology and Education*. Stoke-on-Trent: Trentham Books.

Carroll, J. (2008). Mediated performance: Video production in the English Classroom. In M. Anderson, J. Hughes and J. Manuel (eds), *Drama in the English Classroom* (pp. 175–92). Melbourne: Oxford University Press.

Carroll, N. (1996). *Theorizing the Moving Image*. New York: Cambridge University Press.

Chizhik, A. (2009). Literacy for playwriting or playwriting for literacy. *Education and Urban Society*, 41, 387–409.

Clausen, M. (2008). *Cultural Intersections: A Post-Colonial Approach to Teaching Contemporary Indigenous Australian Theatre*. Unpublished masters thesis, University of Sydney.

Cohen, L. and Manion, L. (2000). *Research Methods in Education*, 4th edn. London: Routledge.

— (2004). *A Guide to Teaching Practice*, 4th edn. London: RoutledgeFalmer.

Connell, W. F., Francis, E. P. and Skilbeck, E. (1957). *Growing up in an Australian City: A Study of Adolescents in Sydney*. Hawthorn: Australian Council for Educational Research.

Cook, H. C. (1917). *The Play Way: An Essay in Educational Method*. London: W. Heinemann.

Coupland, D. (1992). *Generation X : Tales for an Accelerated Culture*. New York: Sphere.

Craft, A. (2002). *Creativity in the Early Years: A Lifewide Foundation*. London: Continuum.

Daley, E. (2003). Expanding the concept of literacy. *Educause Review*, 39(2), 32–40.

Dalrymple, L. (2006). Has it made a difference? Understanding and measuring the impact of applied theatre with young people in the South African context. *Research in Drama Education: The Journal of Applied Theatre and Performance*, 11(2), 201–18.

Deasy, R. J. (2002). *Critical Links: Learning in the Arts and Student Academic and Social Development*. Washington, DC: Arts Education Partnership.

Deasy, R. J. (2004). *Arts Education Partnership: The Arts and Education – New Opportunities for Research*. Retrieved 11 May 2010, from www.gseis.ucla.edu/faculty/files/catterall/catterall

Denzin, N. and Lincoln, Y. (1994). Introduction: Entering the field of qualitative research. In N. Denzin and Y. Lincoln (eds), *Handbook of Qualitative Research*. Thousand Oaks, CA: Sage.

— (eds) (2005). *The Sage Handbook of Qualitative Research*, 3rd edn. Thousand Oaks, CA: Sage.

Dewey J. (1938). *Experience and Education*. New York: Macmillan.

Donelan, K. (2002). Embodied practices: Ethnography and intercultural drama in the classroom. *NJ Drama Australia Journal*, 26(2), 35–44.

— (2005). *The Gods Project: Drama as Intercutltural Education: An Ethnographic Study of an Intercultural Performance Project in a Secondary School*. Nathan, QLD: Griffith University.

Dunn, J. (2003). Linking drama education and dramatic play in the early childhood years. In S. Wright (ed.), *Children, Meaning Making and the Arts* (pp. 117–32). Sydney: Pearson Education.

Dupré, B. (2006). *Creative Drama, Playwriting, Tolerance and Social Justice: An Ethnographic Study of Students in a Seventh Grade Language Arts Class*. Doctoral dissertation. Albuquerque, New Mexico: University of New Mexico.

Durrant, C. and Green, B. (2000). Literacy and the new technologies in school education: Meeting the L(IT)eracy challenge? *Australian Journal of Language and Literacy*, 23(2), 89–108.

Earl, L. (2003). *Assessment as Learning: Using Classroom Assessment to Maximize Student Learning*. Thousand Oaks, CA: Corwin Press.

Eisner, E. (1978). Humanistic trends and the curriculum field. *Journal of Curriculum Studies*, 10(3), 97–204.

— (1999). Does experience in the arts boost academic achievement? *The Clearing House*, 72, 143–9.

— (2002). *The Arts and the Creation of Mind*. New Haven, CT: Yale University Press.

Ely, M. (1991). *Doing Qualitative Research: Circles Within Circles*. New York: Falmer Press.

Enoch, W., Mailman, D. and Beaton, H. (1996). *The 7 Stages of Grieving*, written by Wesley Enoch and Deborah Mailman; dramaturgy by Hilary Beaton. Brisbane, Queensland, Australia: Playlab Press.

Education Queensland (EQ). (2000). *New Basics: Theory into Practice*. Brisbane: EQ.

Ekebergh, M., Lepp, M. and Dahlberg, K. (2004). Reflective learning with drama in nursing education – a Swedish attempt to overcome the theory praxis gap. *Nurse Education Today*, 24(8), 622–8.

Eraut, M. (1995). Developing professional knowledge within a client centred orientation. In T. Guskey and M. Huberman (eds), *Professional Development in Education: New Paradigms and Practices* (pp. 227–52). New York: Teachers College Press.

Eriksson, S. (2009). *Distancing at Close Range: Investigating the Significance of Distancing in Drama Education*. Doctoral dissertation, Abo Academy, Vasa.

Ewing, R. (2010). *Curriculum and Assessment: A Narrative Approach*. Melbourne: Oxford University Press.

Fels, L. (2009). When royalty steps forth: Role drama as an embodied learning system. *Complicity: An International Journal of Complexity and Education*, 6(2), 124–42.

Fischer, G., Giaccardi, E., Eden, H., Sugimoto, M. and Ye, Y. (2005). Beyond binary choices: Integrating individual and social creativity. *International Journal of Human-Computer Studies* (IJHCS), Special Issue on Computer Support for Creativity (edited by E. A. Edmonds and L. Candy), 63(4–5), 482–512.

Fiske, E. (ed.). (1999). *Champions of Change: The Impact of the Arts on Learning*. Washington, DC: The Arts Education Partnership and the President's Committee on the Arts and the Humanities.

Fleming, M., Merrell, C. and Tymms, P. (2004). The impact of drama on pupils' language, mathematics, and attitude in two primary schools. *Research in Drama Education*, 9(2): 177–97.

Floyd, R. (2001). Music gets students better tertiary education. *ASG – The Scholastic*, 4, 3.

Fontana, A. and Frey, J. H. (1994). Interviewing: The art of science. In N. Denzin and Y. Lincoln (eds), *Handbook of Qualitative Research* (pp. 361–76). Thousand Oaks, CA: Sage.

Freebody, K. (2010). Exploring teacher–student interactions and moral reasoning practices in drama classrooms. *Research in Drama Education: The Journal of Applied Theatre and Performance,* 15, 209–25.

Freebody, P. (2003). *Qualitative Research in Education: Interaction and Practice.* London: Sage.

Freebody, P. and Frieberg, J. (2011). Ethnomethodological research in education and the social sciences: Studying 'the business, identities and cultures' of classrooms. In L. Markauskaite, P. Freebody and J. Irwin (eds), *Methodological Choice and Design: Scholarship, Policy and Practice in Social and Educational Research* (pp. 79–92). Dordrecht, Netherlands: Springer.

Friere, P. (1972). *The Pedagogy of the Oppressed.* Harmondsworth: Penguin.

— (2004). *Pedagogy of Hope: Reliving Pedagogy of the Oppressed.* London: Continuum.

Furlong, A. and Cartmel, F. (2009). *Higher Education and Social Justice.* Maidenhead, UK: Open University Press.

Gallagher, K. (2010). Improvisation and education: Learning through? *Canadian Theatre Review,* 143, 42–6.

Gee, J (2007). *What Video Games Have to Teach Us About Learning and Literacy,* Basingstoke: Palgrave Macmillan.

Gibson, R. and Ewing, R. (2006). Integrating the creative arts (with INTEGRITY). *Policy and Practice in Education,* 12(1), 29–43.

Gibson, R. and Anderson, M. (2008). Touching the void: Arts education in australia. *Asia Pacific Journal of Education,* 28(1), 103–12.

Gillies, R. M. (2007). *Cooperative Learning: Integrating Theory and Practice.* Los Angeles: Sage.

Giroux, H. A. (1992). *Border Crossings – Cultural Workers and the Politics of Education.* New York: Routledge, Chapman and Hall.

Goethe J. W. (1833). Denken und Tun. *Maximen und Reflexionen.*

Goldman, S., Booker, A. and McDermott, M. (2007). Mixing the digital, social, and cultural: Learning, identity, and agency in youth participation. *The John D. and Catherine T. MacArthur Foundation Series on Digital Media and Learning* (pp. 185–206). Cambridge: MIT Press.

Goodyear, P. (2000). Environments for lifelong learning: Ergonomics, architecture and educational design, Chapter One in J. M. Spector and T. M. Anderson (eds), *Integrated and Holistic Perspectives on Learning, Instruction and Technology: Understanding Complexity* (pp. 1–18). Dordrecht: Kluwer Academic.

Grady, S. (1996). Toward the practice of theory in practice. In P. Taylor (ed.), *Researching Drama and Arts Education: Paradigms and Possibilities.* London: Falmer Press.

Groundwater-Smith, S., Ewing, R. and Le Cornu, R. (2007). *Teaching: Challenges and Dilemmas.* Victoria, Australia: Thomson.

Gupta, A. S. (2003). Changing focus: A discussion of the dynamics of the intercultural experience. In M. B. a. M. F. Geof Alred (ed.), *Intercultural Experience and Education* (pp. 155–73). Sydney: Mulitlingual Matters.

Hankey, J. (ed.) (2005). *Othello,* 2nd edn. Cambridge: Cambridge University Press.

Hargreaves, A. (2003). *Teaching in the Knowledge Society: Education in the Age of Insecurity.* New York: Teachers College Press.

Harland, J., Kinder, K., Lord, P., Scott, A., Schagen, L. and Haynes, J. (2000). *Arts Education in Secondary Schools: Effects and Effectiveness.* Slough, Australia: National Foundation for Educational Research.

Haseman, B. (2001). The 'Leaderly' process drama and the artistry of 'Rip, Mix and Burn'. Unpublished paper presented at the International Drama in Education Association, Bergen, Norway, International Congress.

Haseman, B., and O'Toole, J. (1986). *Dramawise: An Introduction to the Elements of Drama*. Richmond, VA: Heinemann.

Hatton, C. and Anderson, M. (2004). Devising unities: A recent history of drama education in NSW. In *The State of Our Art. NSW Perspectives in Drama Education* (pp. 3–18). Strawberry Hills, NSW: Currency Press.

Hatton, C. and Anderson, M. (2004). *Dramawise: An Introduction to the Elements of Drama*. Richmond, VA: Heinemann.

Hayes, D., Mills, M., Christie, P. and Lingard, B. (2006). *Teachers and Schooling: Making a Difference – Productive Pedagogies, Assessment and Performance*. Sydney: Allen and Unwin.

Heathcote, D. (1984). Signs and portents. In D. Heathcote, L. Johnson and C. O'Neill (eds), *Dorothy Heathcote: Collected Writings on Education and Drama*. London: Hutchinson.

Heathcote, D., Johnson, L. and O'Neill, C. (1984). *Collected Writings on Education and Drama*. London: Hutchinson.

Heathcote, D. and Bolton, G. (1995). *Drama for Learning: Dorothy Heathcote's Mantle of the Expert Approach to Education*. Portsmouth, NH: Heinemann.

Heppell, S. (2007). Stephen Heppells Weblog. Retrieved 21 March 2009, from www.heppell.net/weblog/stephen/

Herschberg, L. (1997). The man who changed everything. *New York Times Magazine*, p. 116.

Hetland, L. and Winner, E. (2001). The arts and academic achievement: What the evidence shows. Executive Summary. *Arts Education Policy Review*, 102(5), 3–6.

Hodgson, J. (ed.) (1972). *The Uses of Drama*. London: Methuen.

Holland, C. (2009). Reading and acting in the world: Conversations about empathy. *Research in Drama Education: The Journal of Applied Theatre and Performance*, 14(4), 529–44.

hooks, b. (2003). *Teaching Community. A Pedagogy of Hope*. New York and London: Routledge.

Hornbrook, D. (1989). *Education and Dramatic Art,* 2nd edn. London: Routledge.

Hughes, J. (1991). Drama in education: The state of the art; an Australian perspective. In J. Hughes (ed.), *Drama in Education the State of the Art* (pp. 1–11). Sydney: Educational Drama Association.

Janesick, V. (1994). The Dance of Qualitative Research Design: Metaphor, methodolatry and meaning. In N. Denzin and Y. Lincoln (eds), *Handbook of Qualitative Research* (pp. 209–19). Thousand Oaks, CA: Sage.

Jeffrey, B. and Craft, A. (2001). The universalization of creativity. In A. Craft, B. Jeffrey and M. Leibling (eds), *Creativity in Education* (pp. 1–13). London: Continuum.

Jensen, A. P. (2007). *Theatre in a Media Culture: Production, Performance and Perception Since 1970*. Jefferson, NC: McFarland.

Johnson, L. and O'Neill, C. (1984). *Dorothy Heathcote: Collected Writings*. London: Hutchinson.

Johnson, R and Onwuegbuzie, A. (2004). Mixed methods research: A research paradigm whose time has come. *Educational Researcher*, 33(7), 14–26.

Kaiser Family Foundation. (2006). *The Media Family: Electronic Media in the Lives of Infants, Toddlers, Preschoolers, and Their Parents*, Menlo Park, CA: Kaiser Family Foundation.

— (2010). *Generation M2: Media in the Lives of 8- to 18-Year-Olds*. Menlo Park, CA: Kaiser Family Foundation.

Kelly-Byme, D. (1989). *A Child's Play Life: An Ethnographic Study*. New York: Teachers College Press.

Kemmis, S. and McTaggart, R. (2005). Participatory action research. In N. Denzin and Y. Lincoln (eds), *The Sage Handbook of Qualitative Research* (pp. 559–604), 3rd edn. Thousand Oaks, CA: Sage.

Kennedy, G. E., Judd, T. S., Churchward, A., Gray, K. and Krause, K. (2008). First year students' experiences with technology: Are they really digital natives? *Australasian Journal of Educational Technology*, 24(1), 108–22.

Kershaw, B. (1994). Oh, for unruly audiences! or, patterns of participation in twentieth-century. *Drama*, 42(2), 133–54.

— (1994). *Framing the Audience for Theatre. The Authority of the Consumer* (pp. 166–86). Edited by Russell Keat, Nigel Whiteley and Neil Abercrombie. London: Routledge.

— (1999). Oh, for unruly audiences! Or, patterns of participation in twentieth-century theatre. *Modern Drama*, 42(2), 133–54.

Kettley, N. (2010). *Theory Building in Educational Research*. London and New York: Continuum.

McKean, B. (2007). Composition in theater: Writing and devising performance. In Liora Bresler (ed.), *International Handbook of Research in Arts Education* (pp. 503–15). Dordrecht: Springer International Handbooks of Education.

Lave, J. and Wenger, E. (1991). *Situated Learning: Legitimate Peripheral Participation*. Cambridge: Cambridge University Press.

Livermore, J. (ed.). (1998). *More Than Words Can Say: A View of Literacy Through the Arts*. Australia: Australian Centre for Arts Education.

Lovat, T. and Smith, D. (2003). *Curriculum: Action on Reflection*, 4th edn. Sydney: Social Science Press.

Luke, A. and Freebody, P. (1997). Critical literacy and the question of normativity: An introduction. In S. Muspratt, A. Luke and P. Freebody (eds), *Constructing Critical Literacies: Teaching and Learning Textual Practice* (pp. 1–18). St Leonards, NSW: Allen and Unwin.

Mabrito, M. and R. Medley (2008). Why Professor Johnny can't read: Understanding the Net Generation's texts. *Innovate* 4 (6), Retrieved 11 August 2010, from www.innovateonline.info/index.php?view=articleandid=510.

Mahn, H. and John-Steiner, V. (2002). The gift of confidence: A vygotskian view of emotions. In G. Wells and G. Claxton (eds), *Learning for Life in the 21st Century: Sociocultural Perspectives on the Future of Education* (pp. 46–58). Cambridge, MA: Blackwell.

Manuel, J. and Anderson, M. (2008). Assessing drama in English. In Anderson, M., Hughes, J. and Manuel, J. (eds), *Drama and English Teaching: Imagination, Action and Engagement* (pp. 214–223). Melbourne: Oxford University Press.

Marsh, C. J. (1998). *Beginning Drama 11–14*. London: Fulton.

— (2004). *Handbook for Beginning Teachers*, 2nd edn. Frenchs Forest, NSW: Pearson Education Australia.

— (2008). *Handbook for Beginning Teachers Becoming a Teacher*. Frenchs Forest, NSW: Pearson Education Australia.

Marshall, A. (2006). *Each Other: The Drama Classroom and the Cultural Interface*. Paper presented at the Drama Australia 2006, Sydney.

Martello, J. (2002). Four literacy practices roled into one: Drama and early childhood literacies. *Melbourne Studies in Education*, 43(2), 53–63.

McAuley, G. (2000). *Space in Performance, Making Meaning in Theatre*. University of Michigan Press.

McCaslin, N. (2005). Seeking the aesthetic in creative drama and theatre for young audiences. *Journal of Aesthetic Education*, 39(4), 12–19.

McGeogh, K. and Hughes, J. (2009). Digital storytelling and drama: Language, image and empathy. In M. Anderson, D. Cameron and J. Carroll (eds), *Teaching Drama with Digital Technologies* (pp. 113–28). London: Continuum.

Medina, C. L., Weltsek-Medina, G. and Twomey, S. (2007). Critical literacies and Glo/Cal citizenry: Constructing reflective spaces through critical performative pedagogies. *Youth Theatre Journal*, 21(1), 113–28.

Montgomery, K. (2007). *Generation Digital: Politics, Commerce, and Childhood in the Age of the Internet*. Cambridge, MA: MIT Press.

Mooney, M. (1989). *Drama Education in NSW*. Unpublished Master of Arts thesis, Charles Sturt University.

Morgan, N. and Saxton, J. (1987). *Teaching Drama*. London: Hutchinson.

Munns, G. and Woodward, H. (2006). Student engagement and student self-assessment: The REAL framework. *Assessment in Education: Principles, Policy and Practice,* 13(2), 193–213.

National Advisory Committee on Creative and Cultural Education (NACCCE). (1999). *All Our Futures: Creativity, Culture and Education.* NACCCE. Available online at www.dfee.gov.uk/naccce/index1.htm

Neelands, J. (1990). *Structuring Drama Work.* Cambridge: Cambridge University Press.

— (1996). Reflections from an Ivory Tower; Towards an interactive research paradigm. In P. Taylor (ed.), *Researching Drama and Arts Education.* London: Falmer Press.

— (1998). *Beginning drama* 11–14. London: Fulton.

— (1998). Three theatres waiting: Architectural spaces and performance traditions. *NADIE Journal: Selected IDIERI Papers,* 22(1), 10–17.

Neelands, J. (2004). Miracles are happening: Beyond the rhetoric of transformation in the Western traditions of drama education. *Research in Drama Education,* 9(1), 47–56.

Neelands, J. (2009). Acting together: Ensemble as a democratic process in art and life. *RiDE: The Journal of Applied Theatre and Performance,* 14(2), 173–89.

Neelands, J. (2009a). Getting off the subject: English, drama, media and the commonwealth of culture. In J. Manuel, P. Brock, D. Carter, W. Sawyer (eds), *Imagination, Innovation, Creativity: Re-visioning English Education* (pp. 12–19). Sydney: Phoenix Education.

Neelands, J. (2010). Mirror, dynamo or lens? Drama, children and social change. In P. O'Connor (ed.), *Creating Democratic Citizenship through Drama Education.* Stoke-on-Trent, UK: Trentham Books.

Neelands, J. and Goode, T. (2000). *Structuring Drama Work: A Handbook of Available Forms in Theatre and Drama,* 2nd edn. Cambridge: Cambridge University Press.

New London Group (NLG). (1996). A pedagogy of multiliteracies: Designing social futures. *Harvard Educational Review,* 66(1), 69–92.

New South Wales Department of Education and Training. (2003). *Quality Teaching in NSW Public Schools: Starting the Discussion.* Sydney, NSW: Department of Education and Training.

Negroponte, N. (1995). *Being Digital.* New York: Alfred A. Knopf.

Newmann, F. (1996). *Authentic Achievement Restructuring Schools for Intellectual Quality.* San Francisco: Jossey-Bass.

Nicholson, H. (1995). *Performative Acts: Drama, Education and Gender. NADIE Journal,* 19(1), 27–37.

— (2002). The politics of trust: Drama education and the ethic of care. *Research in Drama Education,* 7(1), 81–91.

— (2008). *Applied Drama: The Gift of Theatre.* New York: Palgrave Macmillan

— (2009). *Theatre and Education.* Basingstoke, England: Palgrave Macmillan.

O'Brien, A. and Donelan, K. (2008). *The Arts and Youth at Risk: Global and Local Challenges.* New Castle-Upon-Tyne: Cambridge Scholars.

O'Connor, P. (2010). *Creating Democratic Citizenship through Drama Education: The Writings of Jonothan Neelands* (pp 143–57). Stoke-on-Trent. Trentham Books.

O'Neill, C. (1995). *Drama Worlds: A Framework for Process Drama.* Portsmouth, NH: Heinemann.

O'Neill, C. and Lambert, A. (1982). *Drama Structures. A Practical Handbook for Teachers.* London: Hutchinson.

O'Toole, J. (1992). *The Process of Drama: Negotiating Art and Meaning.* London: Routledge.

O'Toole, J. (1998). Playing on the beach. Consensus among drama teachers – some patterns in the sand. *NADIE Journal,* 22(2), 5–19.

O'Toole, J. (2002). Drama: The Productive Pedagogy. *Melbourne Studies in Education,* 43(2), 39–52.

O'Toole, J. (2006). *Doing Drama Research: Stepping into Enquiry in Drama, Theatre and Education.* Brisbane: Drama Australia.

O'Toole, J., Burton, B. and Plunkett, A. (2005). *Cooling Conflict: A New Approach to Managing Bullying and Conflict in Schools.* Melbourne: Pearson Education.

O'Toole, J. and O'Mara, J. (2007). Proteus, the giant at the door: Drama and theatre in the curriculum. In L. Bresler (ed.), *International Handbook of Research in Arts Education* (pp. 203–18). The Netherlands: Springer.

O'Toole, J., Stinson, M. and Moore, T. (2009). *Drama and Curriculum: A Giant at the Door* Springer [Dordrecht].

Obama, B. (2009). *Speeches.* Available at www.obamaspeeches.com/

Owston, R. (2009). Digital immersion, teacher learning, and games. *Educational Researcher,* 38(4), 270–3.

Oxford English Dictionary (2006). Creativity, noun. *Oxford English Dictionary Online.* Available at www.oed.com. Accessed 28 February 2007.

Paget D. (1987). Verbatim theatre: Oral history and documentary techniques. *New Theatre Quarterly,* 12, 317–36.

Posner, D. (2004). What's wrong with teaching to the test? *Phi Delta Kappan,* 85(10), 749–51.

Postman, N. (1993). *Technopoly: The Surrender of Culture to Technology.* New York: Vintage.

Powell, C. S. (1996). Interview with Jaron Lanier. A cyberspace Renaissance man reveals his current thoughts on the World Wide Web, virtual reality, and other silicon dreams. By Corey S. Powell, *Scientific American,* 15 September 1996.

Prendergast, M. (2008). From guest to witness: Teaching audience studies in post-secondary theatre education. *Theatre Topics,* 18(2), 95–106.

Prensky, M. (2001). Digital natives, digital immigrants. *On the Horizon,* 9(5). Retrieved 10 October 2008, from www.marcprensky.com/writing/Prensky%20-%20Digital%20Natives,%20Digital%20Immigrants%20-%20Part1.pdf

Punch, M. (1994). Politics and ethics in qualitative research. In N. Denzin and Y. Lincoln (eds), *Handbook of Qualitative Research* (pp. 83–98). California: Sage.

Queensland School Restructuring Longitudinal Study (QSRLS). (2001). *School Reform Longitudinal Study: Final Report,* vol. 1. Brisbane: Education Queensland.

Ramsey, G. (2000). *Quality Matters. Revitalising Teaching: Critical Times, Critical Choices.* Sydney: Department of Education and Training.

Raphael, J. (2009). Blogs are better: Encouraging reflection on performance making and drama practice through blogs in M. Anderson, D. Cameron and J. Carroll (eds), *Teaching Drama with Digital Technologies* (pp. 129–48). London: Continuum.

Richardson, L. (1994). Writing: A method of inquiry. In N. Denzin and Y. Lincoln (eds), *Handbook of Qualitative Research* (pp. 516–29). California: Sage.

Robinson, K. (1999). *All our Futures: Creativity, Culture and Education.* London: Department for Education and Employment.

Robinson, K. (2001). *Out of Our Minds : Learning to be Creative.* New York: Capstone: Oxford.

Rushkoff, D. (2005). *Get Back in the Box: Innovation from the Inside Out.* New York: Collins.

Scheurer, P. (1998). The poetic artistry of Cecily O'Neill. In J. Saxton and C. Miller (eds), *Drama and Theatre in Education: The Research of Practice. The Practice of Research* (pp. 30–47). Victoria: IDEA.

Schonmann, S. (2005). 'Master' versus 'Servant': Contradictions in drama and theatre education. *Journal of Aesthetic Education,* 39(4), 31–9.

Schonmann, S. (2007). Appreciation: The weakest link in drama/theater education. In Liora Bresler (ed.), *International Handbook of Research in Arts Education* (pp. 587–600). Dordrecht, The Netherlands: Springer.

Schwandt, T. (2001). *Dictionary of Qualitative Inquiry,* 2nd edn. Thousand Oaks, CA: Sage.

Shulman, L. (1987). Knowledge and teaching. *Harvard Educational Review*, 57(1), 1–22.

Slade, P. (1958). *An Introduction to Child Drama*. London: University of London Press.

Stake, R. (1994). Case studies. In N. Denzin and Y. Lincoln (eds), *Handbook of Qualitative Research* (pp. 435–54). Thousand Oaks, CA: Sage.

Stake, R. (1995). *The Art of Case Study Research*. Thousand Oaks, CA: Sage.

Stake, R. (2000). Case studies. In N. K. Denzin and Y. S. Lincoln (eds), *Handbook of Qualitative Research* (pp. 435–54), 2nd edn. Thousand Oaks, CA: Sage.

Sternberg. R. (2006). The nature of creativity. *Creativity Research Journal*, 18(1), 87–98.

Tauber, A. (1996). *The Elusive Synthesis: Aesthetics and Science*. London: Kluwer.

Taylor, P. (1995). *Pre-Text and Storydrama: The Artistry of Cecily O'Neill and David Booth*. Brisbane: NADIE.

Taylor, P. (2003). *Applied Theatre: Creating Transformative Encounters in the Community*. Portsmouth, NH: Heinemann.

Taylor, P. (2006). Power and privilege: Re-envisioning the qualitative research lens. In J. Ackroyd (ed.), *Research Methodologies for Drama Education* (pp. 1–14). London: Trentham Books.

Taylor, P. (2006). *Assessment in Arts Education*. Portsmouth, NH: Heinemann.

Thompson, J. (1991). Assessing drama: Allowing for meaningful interpretation. In J. Hughes (ed.), *Drama in Education the State of the Art* (pp. 76–82). Rozelle: Educational Drama Association.

Thomson, P. and Sanders, E. (2010). Creativity and whole school change: An investigation of English headteachers' practices. *Journal of Educational Change*, 11(1), 63–83.

UNESCO (2003). Website: http://portal.unesco.org/culture/es/ev.php-URL_ID=29870andURL_DO=DO_PRINTPAGEandURL_SECTION=-465.html UNESCO (2006). Road Map for Arts Education. Retrieved 2 January 2008, from http://portal.unesco.org/culture/en/ev.php-URL_ID=30335andURL_DO=DO_TOPICand-URL_SECTION=201.html

Upitis, R. and Smithrim, K. (2003a). Learning through the arts: National assessment 1999–2000. Final report to the Royal Conservatory of Music. Toronto: The Royal Conservatory of Music.

Veltman, C. (2009). Interview with Mike Leigh. *The Believer Magazine*. Accessed at www.believermag.com/issues/200903/?read=interview_leigh on 10 November 2010

Vygotsky, L. S. (1978). *Mind in Society: The Development of Higher Psychological Process*. Cambridge, MA: Harvard University Press.

Wagner, B. (1976). *Dorothy Heathcote: Drama as a Learning Medium*. London: Hutchinson.

Walker, R. (2003). Teacher development through communities of learning. In D. M. McInerney and S. Van Etten (eds), *Sociocultural Influences and Teacher Education Programs* (pp. 223–46). Greenwich, CT: Information Age.

Watson, K. (2008). Teaching Shakespeare as drama. In M. Anderson, J. Hughes and J. Manuel (eds), *Drama and English Teaching: Imagination, Action and Engagement* (pp. 69–87). Melbourne: Oxford University Press.

Ward, W. (1930). *Creative Dramatics, for the Upper Grades and Junior High School*. New York and London: D. Appleton.

Way, B. (1973). *Development through Drama*. London: Longman.

Wenger, E. (1998). Communities of practice: Learning as a social system. *Systems Thinker*. Retrieved 7 August 2005, from www.co-i-l.com/coil/knowledge-garden/cop/lss. shtml

Wiggins, G. P. (1993). *Assessing Student Performance*. San Francisco: Jossey-Bass.

Wiltshire, K. (2006). In defence of the true values of learning. *The Australian*, 23–24 September, pp. 22–23.

Winston, J. (2010). *Beauty and Education*. New York: Routledge.

Woolland, B. (2008). *Pupils as Playwrights: Drama, Literacy and Playwriting.* Stoke-on-Trent, UK: Trentham Books.

Wright, D. (2005). Reflecting on the body in drama education. *International Drama/Theatre and Education Association and Applied Theatre Researcher,* 6(10).

Wright, M. (1997). *Playwriting in Process.* Portsmouth, NH: Heinemann.

Index

34946101R00099

Printed in Great Britain
by Amazon